GW00858322

Be Aware

Take Care

Tony Willis

What people are saying

Business travelling is getting more and more uncomfortable with increased pressures on time and reduced budgets, especially in the big cities like Berlin, London and Paris. Rushing from one meeting to the next often under significant stress business travellers are especially vulnerable. Advice on how to avoid difficult situations and maintain personal safety in these situations is absolutely essential for today's business community.

Hans-Peter Portner, Global Transition & Transformation Manager

Tony Willis is one of the most diversely trained martial artists in the UK. He has decades of experience both as a practitioner and Instructor. His ability to articulate his experiences with self-protection, and apply them to the business environment is both unique and refreshing. I highly recommend that anyone involved in the business sector and especially business travel - should read his book. It will prove invaluable.

Krishna Godhania, Institute of Filipino Martial Arts

Being a frequent traveller I know the importance of avoiding conflict and Tony Willis has successfully captured the essentials on what to look for and how to act

Magnus Lundgren , Strategic Sales Director Ericsson

This book gives the essential guide for business travellers in self-protection. Tony Willis gives a step by step guide in breaking down essential techniques for close quarter self-defence protection. An essential must for those who wish to protect themselves and their family and Tony gives expert advice for self-protection.

Paul Whitrod, Sifu/Guru/Asan/Ajarn

Over the past 16yrs spent teaching Martial Arts I have been fortunate to meet, teach and learn from some of the most amazing people, one of them being Tony Willis.

Tony possesses the comprehensive knowledge in martial arts to help anyone who wants to learn and become competent in martial arts. One thing that strikes me as amazing is his willingness to learn new skills and to become a white belt again.

I do not only consider Tony a student but also a friend.

I whole-heartedly recommend his training at his 5 Elements facility.

Eddie Kone, 2nd Degree Gracie Jiu-Jitsu Black Belt

If each technique is a brick and every tactic the mortar that binds them then what you build is the true summation of your dedication to Martial Arts: Tony Willis has put in the hours, the days, the years and crafted a fine dojo where the roots are deep.

Pat O'Keeffe, Author & Senior Martial Arts Instructor

I don't think we realise the amount of people that experience stress and conflict while travelling and it can be mentally, physically and emotionally challenging.

Tony has come up with a fantastic idea writing this book. I'm sure it will be helpful to a lot of business travellers and the general public.

Dev Barrett, Fmr WAKO Full Contact World Champion, 7th Degree Black Belt, Head of ECKA

Acknowledgments

For many years I have toyed around with the idea of writing a book and now this my first is out with another 2 already in the pipeline. I would therefore like to thank my business coach David Holland MBA who has motivated me to finally do what I had been meaning to do for so long.

I would also like to thank all those throughout my career and martial arts training that have helped me including my late father who inspired me to continue to strive to be the best I can.

From the Martial Arts World I would like to pay particular thanks to the following.

Please note that I have removed their titles for ease of reading for those not involved in martial arts. Names are in alphabetical order.

Dev Barrett, Krishna Godhania, Pat O'Keeffe, Eddie Kone, Paul Whitrod

About the Author

Tony Willis MBA FCMI is Founder & Head Coach of 5 Elements, training individuals, colleges and corporations in achieving goals, self-protection and martial arts.

What makes this book different from many self-defence books is that it is built around Tony's understanding of delivering at a senior level in the corporate sector. For many years Tony worked at a senior level for large corporations regularly travelling on business. That travel coupled with forty years of martial arts and self-defence training was the foundation for this book.

While working as a Director at one organisation he achieved one of his goals of being the expert interviewed by the analysts on the stock market following the release of the annual report.

In 2000 Tony achieved another of his goals of visiting the Great Wall of China while studying traditional Chinese Medicine in Beijing.

Today Tony spreads his time between continuing his own training, coaching and managing the 5 Elements Academy and delivering presentations and courses in the corporate sector.

Tony has held NATO and London's Met Police security clearance.

Forward

This book is all about understanding and managing risk.

As businessmen we understand the concept of risk and can relate to it so make sure you apply it to your life as well as your latest venture or project

The whole approach of our self-protection and self-defence training is the following premise. Read it don't skip this vital statement to get to the meet of the book, think on it over and over again. Nothing else matters.

Nothing absolutely nothing is worth more than your life and the lives of your loved ones.

If I asked you how much you would be willing to pay for your life what would you say, a million, 10 million, everything you had.

So why would you risk fighting a mugger over a £100 watch, or £10 in your wallet.

Now ask the same question after you fought back and were stabbed in the liver, laying on a cold wet street slowly fading away thousands of miles from home and your loved ones. What price would you pay now? What if you could go back and change things, what would you do now? Nothing absolutely nothing is worth more than your life and the lives of your loved ones.

I really can't emphasise this enough. Peoples ego gets in the way far too often. How many times have you opened a newspaper and seen someone killed stopping a burglary or trying to stop someone taking their car or gold watch. Its unjust unfair and completely wrong that someone comes along and takes your stuff but nevertheless it is not worth risking serious injury or death to prevent it.

If at all possible don't ever put yourself in the position where you test your survival skills and ability to fight. You may win a hundred times but if you lose once then that may be the final chapter. Make sure your pride doesn't leave your loved ones without a husband/wife or parent.

This isn't a martial arts book it's a book for business and regular travellers. Hopefully it will help you in recognising and understanding risk.

Contents

Dedication

To my ever supportive and amazing wife who somehow manages to put up with me – Kellie Willis

Fear

In no way do we want the business traveller or any other traveller to turn into a paranoid worrier constantly looking over their shoulder and worrying about what's around the next corner.

The aim is to give you some simple advice and tips on how to identify and assess risk and then put in place action plans to help ensure people can work efficiently and effectively and then get home to their loved ones safely.

This book is about recognising and understanding some basic principles, its purpose is to provoke you to recognise possible risks and provoke you to think about and plan how to manage that.

In principle Business travel is no different to any other travel such as the regular vacations taken by thousands of people as they take their annual breaks. However business travel is different in that for some they may be taking a large number of flights and trips to areas that they don't know and the frequency is much higher. For some it's not uncommon to be taking two flights in a single day.

So it's a bit like rolling the dice, if I roll the dice once it's got a 1 in 6 chance of landing on a 6. Now although the odds stay the same if I roll it 100 times it's very unlikely that in all those rolls I will never once roll a 6.

Additionally some areas are notoriously difficult for travellers and some others that we feel are safe are actually very loaded for risk. Now I have no great desire to upset certain cities or regions of the world but if for instance you have sat in the departure lounge at some cities then you will almost certainly be witnessing travellers talking about being robbed or assaulted during their stay.

I remember sitting in Barcelona airport after having a fantastic time there with my wife reflecting on our visit. We did all the usual tourist things as well as the business side and were robbed of our camera while sitting at a café in Las Ramblas. Now for me it was a great learning experience as of course I had followed none of the advice I give everyone else. This false confidence can be the downfall of so many.

Not only was I not listening to my own advice my ego was on full tilt so that I continued to ignore my guidance and recovered the camera which although it had some nice pictures reflecting our memories on was certainly not worth the potential of my wife attending my funeral. Fortunately I survived unscathed but this hammers home the message I give throughout this book, presentations and courses I give. Nothing is of enough value to risk your safety unless it's to save the life of yourself or a loved one.

You need to also recognise that fear is not only an emotional response it's a chemical response to events as well.

Adrenaline flows through the body causing reactions and the fight or flight response. Many of us use these physical processes and reactions every day in our work. Anyone who has stood at large conferences and given presentations or speeches will recognise that nervous buzz you get.

For some it makes them want to turn and run as far from the podium as possible, for others, although they also get that feeling it energises them to get up there and they enjoy that feeling.

Directors get that buzz when launching a make or break new product and project managers get it when they are about to handover to the customer for the first time.

Recognise that adrenaline can be a big advantage in life, don't treat it as a sign of panic, learn to harness it so you can truly shine.

Principles

As in everything that we learn self-protection should be about understanding and appreciating certain principles. If all we learn is techniques then when something new or different comes along we don't know what to do and don't have the techniques and tools in place to deal with it. However running through scenarios is a good idea and isn't the same as only having techniques. Scenarios can be great for working through potential issues in a group or team environment and fit really well in a corporate setting.

If we think of a project, we want the project manager to understand how he can use the tools they have learned and adapt to different situations. So for example many times across projects they will have seen problems with physical assets being delivered on time but it's highly unlikely that they have received specific training on what to do if a truck delivering the items crashes 1 mile away and the equipment is destroyed. What the project manager does is utilise the principles they have learnt both formerly and through experience to get the project back on track.

Applying this in the context of self-protection and at the risk of upsetting some of my martial arts colleagues in my experience many self-defence courses are in all honestly poorly taught with set attacks and set defences against those attacks being demonstrated.

Now in theory there isn't anything inherently wrong with that **IF** the instructor is accompanying that with guidance on the principals involved.

A great example of what I am discussing here is for the attacker to grab you with their right hand and then you do defence xyz. Well what if they grab you with the other hand or they hold their thumb down instead of thumb up. Then the techniques you just learned don't work too well if at all. This is a crazy situation as you would have to be an expert in thousands of possible techniques and that's simply not possible.

When the sessions are taught well and the student understands the principles then if the attacker uses their right hand and not their left for example the same principles can be adapted to work with little thought.

No one does what you expect them to do when you expect them to do it, if only life were that easy.

Nothing is worth anything to you other than your life or the life of your loved ones.

Don't fight a mugger for a £10 or £1000 watch and get killed. Get away safe and buy a new one on the insurance money

Principle 1

Everything we do carries risk

If we adopt or at least recognise and understand a set of principles then we can understand and this gives us the opportunity to asses and manage the risk.

Don't forget everything has risk. If we walk out the door in the morning there is risk, we could get hit by lightning or run down by a stray vehicle, it's unlikely but there is always that risk. However if we did nothing and stayed in bed for the day then that in itself carries risk, the house might catch fire, we might suffer bed sores or get clogged arteries through lack of activity.

Recognising that everything has risk and that it's not just about avoiding risk but recognising, understanding and formulating plans to address it using the principles we learn is what makes a difference. We do this constantly throughout every day of our lives anyway. It's just that this has become so familiar and common place that we don't recognise that we are doing this. When we are a small child we have it drummed into us how to stop at the roadside and carefully assess what's going on and the risks before we cross the road. Look left then right then left again and don't cross between parked cars. As adults we subconsciously continue to do much of this but not as separate events just as part of what we do when we get to a road.

Self-protection follows many of the principles we all use every day either as entrepreneurs, directors or employees. While we work, motivate ourselves and or others to deliver the best they can, plan, budget, design or deliver a business we formulate plans to manage risk. Each individual at any given time has a level of risk that they work with, we don't stop developing new products or delivering the products we have just because there is a risk involved. We try and identify risks and plan either consciously or sub consciously to avoid or overcome those risks. It's important we understand this principle as it means we avoid becoming paranoid and overplay all the risks around us to an extent that we can no longer enjoy life. Please remember enjoying life to the full is not without risk itself but its worth striving for as an objective.

This constant identification of risk, recognition and planning goes on continuously without us recognising it in the most part. Only when it's a really significant issue or calculation does it rise to our conscious level of thinking.

Principle 2

Transitions from one state to another carry the biggest risk as there are more unknowns.

Every time something changes we have to reconsider and recalculate the risk.

If driving a car we can recognise and understand the risks but once I stop and start to get out of the car transitioning from one environment to another we instinctively observe, evaluate and recognise the new as previously unknown risks around us.

This is absolutely key in self-protection.

If we think through an average day then we can recognise that the whole day is made up of sections joined together by transitions. To explain this let's look at a couple of quick and easy scenarios that work well in explaining this.

As we open the front door we go from a recognised safe comfortable state to possibly being slightly blinded by the sudden change of light and sound that comes immediately we open that door. At this point you are at your most vulnerable.

As you leave the tube or underground station look at everyone around you, some shield their eyes due to the change in light others immediately light a cigarette or are head down looking at their mobile. These are transitions. A perfect opportunity for the mugger or worse.

Principle 3

Not everyone is out to get you in fact 99.99999% are probably just like you and would probably help you back to your feet even if you simply tripped up.

However somewhere out there a lion is stalking their prey looking to split the unwary or weaker animal from the herd so they can take them down.

Transitions

If you think through the average day that you have and consider the transitions that occur it's a considerable amount.

All of the different segments of the day are transitions.

If you break your day down into chunks of events then between each one is a transition. Imagine you were a producer putting a video or PowerPoint together of your day. You would film the different segments and then between each one add a fade or interweave so each segment joins together this makes the whole movie rather than having individual scenes. This in your case joins each part of your day together into the whole day.

In self-protection these transitions are your times of biggest risk.

It can sometimes be hard to recognise why transitions are so vital but they really are. The art comes in recognising when we are moving from one scene to the next and that this transition is of vital importance in maintaining your safety.

Consider watching or imaging from a novel and picturing a bodyguard for the president of the USA on the TV evening news. When are they most alert and in action, it's the transitions. The time of the president leaving a building to getting into a car etc.

If you don't quite understand this look up the shooting of former President Ronal Reagan and you will see the impact of transitions and how they can be used against you in reality.

During transitions the risks are amplified because of the sheer number of unknown variables. These unknown elements can possibly become your weakness. For example if you step out of your car you go from a warm familiar environment with tinted windows and heated seats to an unknown street. In the street the noise, light and people around you are all out of your control. The sun might shine in your face someone you don't know could be walking up behind you or a loud noise might distract you.

The transition itself in not the issue it's the fact that you need to react to those transitions. During each of the transitions there is a catch up period where you are consciously or subconsciously evaluating events and your environment and making decisions on the results. In my opinion what makes us so impressive as human beings is that all of this goes on constantly without us even thinking about it.

One of the things that is important here is the amount of variables there are that are outside your control.

Some Key transitions during your average business day

- Leaving home in the morning
- Boarding a train
- Arriving at the destination station
- Entering the office building
- Popping out to meet a client
- Taxi to the airport

- Arriving at the airport
- The destination airport
- Entering the office buildings
- Taxi to the airport
- Arriving at the destination airport
- Taxi home
- Entering your house

Now, just for a minute, close your eyes and imagine that you were a kidnapper and your normal self was the target. At what point would you grab yourself. When were you an easy target, not sure of where you were or distracted.

That's when you are most at risk, at those points. It doesn't have to be the risk of kidnap it could be anything at all from having your pockets picked to being assaulted but if you think about it even though you have no training or experience you already know the issues.

Preparation even in small doses can make significant differences. For instance consider these two different scenarios

1. You stop at the door, open your briefcase or handbag and start searching for your keys. When you find them you fumble for the correct key, open the door and enter.
2. You briefly check over your shoulder as you approach your house checking you aren't being followed, you arrive at the door with the correct key in your hand, alert to your surroundings open the door and check behind you while entering.

In the first scenario you don't give yourself the opportunity to carry on walking past your property if someone was following you. You stop at the door for vital minutes unaware of what's going on around you and you give a possible intruder the opportunity to approach and bundle you through the door as you enter. Alternatively as you fumble unaware for your keys they could simply take your bag and head off.

These simple regular situations mirror and repeat themselves constantly throughout your working or leisure days. During these transitions from one situation to another is when you are most at a significant risk. Think how easy it would be to follow you and rob you at the time you wait at the door maybe sheltering in the dark from the rain. Worse you could be kidnapped, dragged inside the premises and robbed or attacked. It sounds dramatic but think of being in the attacker's shoes, how simple it would be to casually walk along the road and follow the person to their door, you could be on top of them overpowering them in seconds.

Imagine fumbling for your keys as an attacker takes the 3 quick steps to close the distance between you punches you in the face and runs off with your bag. For many that is a devastating and traumatic event but in reality that isn't too bad an assault it could be much worse.

Take for example the underground or rail trip you make every day as part of your commute. One of the biggest transitions you will see in action is during times of mass movement. We act like pack animals sometimes and adopt the norms of what is happening around us. Check out a train arriving. Suddenly a mass of people all arrive and leave the station. This move from dark areas, lit but completely different to sunlight, is when people look down to avoid the light, look at their smartphone for maps or messages and light a cigarette. All these distracted people are easy pickings for someone to follow or steal the smartphone.

Mixed amongst the mass throng of people two pickpockets would move seamlessly undetected by the majority of people. Changing items between each other or another accomplice, even if caught by the police, they may no longer have any items in their possession at that time.

In the UK it's easy to think in terms of pickpockets as it's something that we can relate to but remember in some countries and instances this mass movement from a train could hide much more serious consequences such as kidnap or abduction.

Possessions

Wallets and passports

I have grouped these two items together. From my own personal experience I believe that if you have a wallet with credit cards, hopefully including a company card and a passport you can travel and purchase just about anything you need.

Passports are vital for travellers so the loss of one can be enough to cause you serious delay and inconvenience at best. Depending where you are in the world it's possible that it could result in you being temporarily detained until you are able to make contact with your embassy. Many countries allow business passengers to obtain a second passport, in the UK this is possible if your company justifies the reason for doing so.

There may be a variety of reasons in addition to the convenience that you would like a second passport. For instance if you travel to Israel on business it has been reported that you may have difficulty getting into some other countries if your passport is stamped. However since 2013 the immigration authorities have issued entry cards which you keep with your passport until you leave.

If travelling you should have more than one credit card. It's easy to get another credit card so if you don't have more than one or you only take your company card on business trips then change this so you have a spare. Many banks sometimes make the error of reacting to an international transaction flag on their fraud detection system by suspending the card. That in itself is enough reason to carry more than one card. This has happened to me on several occasions with one helpful bank not only suspending that particular card but all my other cards I had with them including my business account. The fact I was just about to check out of the hotel in Bangkok didn't particularly help with my levels of frustration.

So while travelling the plan is to use two wallets each with a credit card in. One of the wallets will be your dummy wallet and the other your real wallet. It's important that your dummy wallet appears genuine so if it only has a few dollars or pounds in its unlikely to fulfil the role.

If mugged you simply give over the dummy wallet, if it has a credit card and a reasonable amount of cash in its likely that they may be satisfied with that. Although you have lost the card and cash you still have another one so the inconvenience is significantly reduced.

If you are the victim of pickpockets with luck they will take one not both wallets.

If I'm travelling I like to have a spare card in the hotel safe as a backup but then I like to be as sure as I can. You might not be as risk adverse as I am.

Your luggage

(Includes hand luggage)

Before you get to the airport remove any old stickers or tags from your luggage, don't identify yourself to the crowds as a frequent traveller.

Frequent travellers have a number of potential problems and if at all possible you want to hide this fact from everyone else. There are many reasons for this but just look at a simple scenario to help explain.

Did that taxi driver who took you to the station strike up a casual conversation about what you were doing and why you had a suitcase?
Did they notice your gold loyalty travel card attached to your bag?
Is it the same cab company that has picked you up ten times this month?

Well maybe they aren't criminal's maybe they just moan about how lucky you are to be travelling away all the time to that guy in the bar. Maybe he is the one who visits your home and takes what he wants while you are away, or maybe he is also honest but mentions the conversation to the guy in the takeaway who isn't.

Oh and please don't use those travel tags that some cases have so you can add your name and address in case your bags get lost. Why advertise that your home is empty for the next few days or weeks.

Most baggage tags supplied at the airline desks have barcodes on that are scanned as they progress through the conveyor belts. Modern systems have these codes checked for times as well to ensure that baggage is not taken aside for either theft or terrorist reasons. Anyone who travels frequently will have lost some baggage somewhere but that little tag with your home address on isn't going to make a significant difference. If you weigh the risk against reward it simply doesn't make sense to advertise that you are absent from that home address.

I will constantly go back to this point again and again, get insurance. If for some reason your employer does not fully cover you on your business travel then often your home contents insurance covers you for more than you would realise but if not get a good travel insurance.

Why do we discuss insurance surely that's irrelevant to self-protection?

Well in a way you are right however it's a psychological switch that we are attempting to turn on. The aim of insurance isn't to get everything back the purpose of insurance is so you can relax, knowing that if things go wrong you are financially covered. Now remember back to the opening statement in the book. We said nothing apart from your life was worth fighting for. With the knowledge that you have insurance to cover everything anyway that fear switch has just subconsciously been turned. As a result you are more inclined to let things be taken rather than risking you safety. At the back of your mind is the thought of so what, I can claim it all back anyway.

The leaflet or magazine scam

This can be used in lots of different locations such as cafes, restaurants, trains, more or less anywhere there is a table that people place their valuables such as phones, tablets and cameras.

I fell victim to this one while relaxing at a street side table watching the world go by. It was hot and we had been really busy as usual so were taking a few minutes downtime to recover. If my wife hadn't recognised the scam we would have lost our camera, as it was I had to go and retrieve it (Not something I would ever recommend).

The idea of the scam is very simple and I believe that at least in some cases the café owners also know this is going on. I find it very hard to believe that with this happening all the time they would allow people to walk through giving out leaflets in this way without warning customers otherwise.

The basic principle to the scam is that someone comes up to you in a hustler pushy way with leaflets in their hand asking if you are interested in whatever is on the leaflet. They know you won't be interested that's the idea but they put some leaflets on the table in front of you anyway. As they are a bit pushy most people wave them away, they simply pick up their leaflets and go. What's interesting is that they normally don't go to the next table they simply walk away. That in itself is strange, if you were selling something why not got to every table. A few minutes later you can't find your phone, even at this stage some people don't work out what just happened.

That's ok its part of the scam, why should you recognise a scam you aren't a street hustler. What they did was lay their leaflets on top of your phone/wallet/camera and as they walked off they picked up their leaflets plus your valuables.

When this happened to me I was fortunate that he didn't hand off the stolen camera to an accomplice which is a common tactic for hustlers like this. As he walked away he did take his jacket off so he went from someone in a bright blue jacket to someone in a grey top. Luckily I was after him by then and saw the changeover. As I mentioned before following and confronting someone like this is both stupid and careless but luckily I got away with making a big mistake like that.

Cashpoint

If you need cash then the local bank cashpoints are often used. One of the great advantages of cashpoints of course is that you can travel the world cashless these days and just get local currency at any cashpoint. Long gone in the distant past is the idea of travellers cheques, in fact when I gave a recent presentation none of the younger people in the audience had a clue what they were. I think on the most part they have been consigned to history along with the idea of having film in your camera.

As regular travellers it's great to be able to simply arrive in country and be able to get local cash so easily. If your PA or office change plans and you end up going to Singapore instead of Boston as planned then it's no problem as far as the cash goes. Cash and a couple of credit cards along with a passport mean that you are truly free to travel the globe.

Of course everything this convenient has a negative to it. We sometimes forget how much technology like this has revolutionised the way we live. However along with every new idea someone somewhere is working out how to create a fraud or low level crime such as theft from each change. Having previously run a major fraud department it amazed me how clever some of these people were. There really is no better advert to the local low life than someone stood at a cashpoint. "Sorry I don't have any cash" will no longer wash they just saw you draw out a wad of notes. I have simply lost count of the amount of beggars I have seen across the globe sitting at the side of a cashpoint machine.

There are basically two major designs of cashpoint machines. There are those based in a room normally as part of a bank but sometimes in shopping malls where you swipe your card to gain entry. The second type is often simply referred to as hole in the wall machines. As this suggests they are just fixed to

the side of a wall outside banks, garages and shops.

Neither offers you the protection of people not realising you are gathering cash. If you are simply making a deposit then you should assume that bystanders believe you have just withdrawn cash.

There are several ways we can look at these different setups as each has advantages and disadvantages for you.

If we look at the cashpoints in the context of assault the room based systems have a slightly improved security as in theory everyone in there has swiped their card to gain entry and they are always well covered by cameras. However it's possible a stolen card could be used to gain entry so you shouldn't lower your guard. Additionally if there is any kind of robbery or confrontation you are then trapped in this locked room with your attacker. Even a well-meaning passer-by can't come to your aid and assistance. CCTV is great in helping the police catch who ever robbed, raped or murdered you after the event but never rely on CCTV to protect you before or during your struggles.

If you are in one of these types of areas with cashpoints and someone knocks on the door asking to be let in what would you do?

Think first act later.

If they were able to use the machines then their card would also open the door and let them in. The fact they want you to help them enter means that they can't use the machines anyway. If that doesn't raise alarm bells with you then it should. One of the ways that these types of characters fool you into letting them in is by having something in their hands like shopping bags or being on the phone. These are all distractions to take your mind off the fact they can't get entry into the area means they shouldn't be in there. At this point even if you don't let them in you should be really alert as they may well be waiting outside.

The hole in the wall machines offer you the chance to just leave the card and cash and run. Yes you will be down a few notes but really it isn't worth fighting over. Remember what we said at the beginning if I asked you what you would pay to be able to get home that night it would be far more than is hanging out the cashpoint at that time.

Think again, imagine you had fought back and been stabbed in the liver and were currently bleeding to death laying on a cold wet street thousands of miles away from home and your loved ones and I was able to ask how much you would pay for all of that to not have happened what would you offer to pay then.

The biggest danger from the hole in the wall option is that someone approaches unnoticed and blindside you. In this scenario you don't have the option to run or just hand over the cash as you have already been hit, stabbed or shot. Awareness around you at all times is crucial. When I talk about awareness I don't mean to start looking around constantly like a startled hare as it identifies you as a victim. Additionally if you were watching a cashpoint and someone was really nervous then you and everyone will assume they are drawing out large sums.

A little tip here is that some cashpoint machines deliberately have a mirrored surface at about head height allowing you to keep glancing up and being able to see behind you. If you feel someone is watching or too close then cancel the transaction make a fuss of looking mad shake your head and stride off. People will assume you were refused the cash and simply wait for the next unsuspecting victim.

Shoulder surfing and a number of other similar scams have inevitably sprung up to take advantage of these cash machines. Your main defence is to be alert to your surroundings and other people. If someone talks to you while you are working the machine assume the worst. This is an intrusion into your personal space and if it isn't setting off alarm bells for you then nothing will.

When giving a talk I was asked about what I would recommend in the situation where someone was forced to go to a cashpoint and withdraw money.

In this case the person was coerced by a gang with a weapon being used to threaten them. All situations are different and in most there is probably not a right or wrong that you can state as each person and each attacker will behave in different ways. Couple that with the environment around them and as events unfold circumstances, threats and levels of danger could change rapidly.

My overwhelming recommendation for the majority of people in this type of situation is to give the people the money they want. If possible take any opportunity to make good your escape but not at risk of your own safety.

This type of theft has a natural ending to it, its time defined in that you can only withdraw so much money before your card is no longer of use. You and your attacker both know that and that is a huge problem.

As the events come to a natural conclusion the attacker is left with a problem and that problem is you. They have a choice to make now which may have already been decided weeks or months ago when this was being planned. Do they let you go or do they make sure you can't talk about what happened to the authorities which could lead to their arrest. The likelihood of each choice is not linear and could depend on a number of variables some of which you don't know.

Depending on where you are in the world taking someone's life might be a lot less of a major decision than elsewhere.

Travel

At an airport - where is it safe to meet or grab a coffee?

So once again we are off on our latest trip to visit another office, customer or supplier. You don't have to be an airline gold card holder to be travelling extensively on business. Although video conference, Skype and email may have affected many business travellers it's still without doubt useful to meet people face to face to create a close working relationship.

Humans are at core animals and the face to face bond created between business partners can often carry you through a number and range of difficult situations. When you are pulling everything out of the bag to ensure that critical project delivers on time its often personal bonds built up between colleagues and partners that provides the additional 10% needed.

Updates and follow ups can be OK on Skype but it won't build the bond that people have used for centuries to create and develop that instinctive tie that we partly rely on to create trust and understanding.

When you arrive at the airport the entrance hallways in most modern airports are full of shops, fast food outlets and coffee shops way before we need to be finding the boarding pass to go through to airside (that part after security).

If for example you go into Heathrow the entrances in all the terminals are lined with shops and restaurants. Now it's very tempting after a track across town and if you have spare time to want to collapse and grab a coffee and it's also a great place to meet colleagues.

Even frequent travellers who have loyalty cards from BA, Star Alliance or one of the other airlines and have access to their business lounges often meet colleagues in a coffee shop prior to going through to the lounge.

So the question comes with the recent upsurge in security awareness where exactly are we most exposed and where are we most likely to be safer.

Well just think for a minute, identify and evaluate the risks.

When you walk in the airport terminal it's usually packed with people from a large number of countries and normally under a high police presence.

There is good reason for that.

The vast majority of people in the terminal on the public side have bags and luggage and none of them have been through any security checks. Coupled with that there are a lot of people in a confined area which is about as big a security problem as you can imagine.

To reduce the risk considerably avoid queues and get airside as soon as possible. Airside basically means once you are through the security screening.

As a business traveller you probably have access to a lounge and if so arrange to meet colleagues there but if not arrange to meet them once you have passed through security.

Although airports themselves always remain high on the list of targets of various terrorist type groups mainly because of the publicity and impact they can have being airside is one of the few area in public where everyone around you has been through a security check.

Many airports outside across the world have no clear separation between arrivals and departures. This means that the clear barrier between those about to board a plane and those just in the airport or just arrived does not exist. Some airports only having security checks at the gate with the rest of the airport being unchecked.

You should be aware however that often at this point everyone has a boarding pass so some level of filtering has occurred even though it's not as high.

If in this type of airport spend as much time in the business lounge and sitting at the gate past security as possible.

What you are basically attempting to do is manage your risk. The biggest risk is due to the fact that there are a large number of people with large bags. Terrorists know this and they also know how much publicity they get from an explosion or attack at a major airport. As a result the further you can get from the majority of people who have not been through security checks the safer you are.

Arrival at the destination airport

If I was to give one piece of advice to anyone going to a destination airport for the first time it would be to arrange collection before you set off.

Most airports in Europe and the USA are actually quite easy to navigate and find a taxi. However it's so easy to arrive at an airport you are unfamiliar with and be collected as you leave the arrival gate that I would always recommend it.

For those travelling further afield I would most certainly arrange collection. If you are unfamiliar with airports in the Far East or Africa then it's a must have on arrival. I remember arriving in Beijing, and Ho Chi Min and being swamped with touts trying to get you to use their transport.

From my experience Beijing hasn't been beaten for taxi touts. Arriving off a long flight and being swamped with people can be a very unnerving experience even for the seasoned traveller. On another note just think how easy it is to pick your pocket as everyone bustles around you.

Being unfamiliar with a country, language, culture or currency all put you at a huge disadvantage. Couple that with a long flight and you really are at risk.

The Hotel

On arriving at the hotel reception desk there are a couple of situations which happen repeatedly and you really want to avoid.

The missing bag

As we get to the desk we put our laptop bag or briefcase down beside our case and start explaining to the receptionist who we are.

It's an everyday occurrence and most of us are fairly relaxed as we are now in a hotel environment, have travelled and are seeking 10 minutes of comfort and relaxation before a busy work schedule of meetings etc. cuts in.

At that point the laptop bag is picked up and off it goes, not only with your laptop in but also your notes business cards, schedule etc. That might sound farfetched but from personal experience I can say that with a couple of hundred staff travelling this happened quite frequently. Think of the risk to the thief. It's very limited, if caught they simply apologise saying they thought it was theirs and wander off. Dressed in a suit and talking to the reception desk why should anyone challenge them.

It's not the cost of the missing laptop it's the information it holds. Even if there is nothing sensitive or commercially confidential on the laptop it's your work, your notes your information. Keeping everything backed up is obviously helpful but remember your notepad and iPad holds your thoughts as well as the files you safely backup.

The Helpful Receptionist

*Hello MR Smith your room is number 452 and you
will be staying with us for 3 nights*

- They just announced to the 30 people gathered
around reception.

That's the prompt to leave reception and return
quietly half hour later and ask for a change of room
and ask that they don't announce it to anyone who
could overhear.

Sounds a bit exaggerated and why make an issue of
something so simple? Well let's see what could be
happening here.

We have no idea who overheard the statement

We don't know if someone in the vicinity would like
to rob or harm us

For travellers including female travellers who are
alone this is a risk that you simply don't need and is
completely unnecessary

Although unlikely it's possible the receptionist is
involved in a scam of some kind and has just
signalled their accomplice that you are to be the
victim that day.

As a standard traveller this is bad enough however if
you are at high risk of kidnap due to your status or
business then this is critical and you should change
hotel immediately. See the information in the chapter
on catastrophic instances for more regarding kidnap.

The hotel room

It's easy to revert to our simple animal behaviours and start to treat your hotel room as your home and castle. Relaxing and believing that it's your sanctuary and that you are safe and secure with the rest of the world excluded outside that locked door.

Please remember there are any number of people that could have access quite legitimately to your room. This is not your home where hopefully you carefully look after each set of your keys. It's a business where a large number of people need to have access to customer's rooms. If you then add the fact that some people who shouldn't be able to have access probably do then you can see that this isn't your private sanctuary at all. It's a false sense of security that quickly envelopes you in its warmth lulling you into making simple mistakes that you would otherwise not make.

Again remember nothing is risk free and just because there are risks doesn't mean that you shouldn't accept them just be aware, recognise them and plan accordingly.

The majority of business or casual travellers will travel extensively throughout their life and never experience a serious problem. Just try and stack the odds so that is the experience you have as well.

Hotel keys

Hotel keys are as varied as the types of hotel. Many modern hotels have moved to swipe cards or plastic key cards of some kind or another. As we go forwards it's likely that these will become virtual keys with some already experimenting with iPhone keys.

One of the initial drivers for the move away from old style conventional metal keys was that customers kept losing them. For those that have had these keys I'm sure you will remember some hotels being quite creative in helping prevent this by fitting large fobs such as a lump of wood. There is additionally a security problem with mechanical keys in that it's possible for a guest to get a copy of the key made.

The advantage of swipe or computer based cards is that the key automatically expires once along with the departure date. The key itself has no reference features such as number to tie it to a specific room so even if it's lost in the foyer it isn't much use to any would be thief.

Additionally they are very cost effective and easy to replace when the guests lose them

Card Keys

Let's look at three things you didn't know about the Hotel Plastic Card Key

1. The room card key does not hold all your guest information

For many years since the introduction of the card key there has been some concern that the key card you get at a hotel reception holds all your personal guest information. This simply isn't true in a reputable hotel. The key holds a room number and code that identifies the card to the room. In coming years this technology itself will be replaced as room keys working on mobile devices have been available for the past couple of years. The card does not hold your credit card details.

2. I'm a business traveller on my own I only need one key

Take the opportunity to have another card, if the first one wasn't slid into the programmer correctly you get a second chance to have a keycard that works without returning to reception. You can then get the faulty card reset next time you pass the reception desk

3. Use that second card

If you have one of the fittings on the wall in your room that trigger the lights and sometimes the TV from the keycard then use that second card to leave it in the slot when you are away from the room, at night or after the room has been made up.

Yes we know that's not very environmentally green but it's a great little safety tip. If someone checks your room is unoccupied they will believe there is someone in the room as the lights and equipment is all on.

If you don't have a room where the electric is operated by a keycard then leave the lights and TV on when you go out at night. If you leave it on during the day the maid will simply turn it off so it has limited use.

If you are in a business hotel with a turn down service or more expensive hotel with butler service then they will often leave lights on for you anyway so don't worry about leaving them on in an evening when you go out.

The hotel layout, stairs and hallways

When checking out your room one of the things you should firstly check is the approach and any side doors. Most hotel hallways have a couple of entrances and exits including escalators, stairways and fire exits.

As you look at the door to your room you will be able to see the visual approach both to your own door and also consider the reverse view looking out from your door. Some older or more expensive hotels will have lots of twists and turns, side hallways and doors setback. This can make the hotel seem more exclusive and more boutique rather than the standard simple layout. From a protection point of

view this results in interrupted vision to and from your own doorway.

If you can't see your doorway as you approach it means that it's impossible to identify any possible risks. There is the possibility that someone could be waiting by your door, this could be significant or not but you won't be able to gather information to make that decision. This means that if you feel uncomfortable you can't just past the door. If you have already checked out the layout of the floor you will know if walking past your room without raising suspicion would be possible.

Locking your room

Remember I said earlier your room is not your castle.

If you look at your room or suite that you are staying in and then ask yourself if you would like to be trapped in there with someone who was seeking to harm you. The answer should be no so that should make you recognise that you should always lock the room and start using the latch or deadbolt when in the room.

Most hotel rooms have a double locking method. The locking that I personally prefer is the dual lock of an automatic door lock associated with a keycard, of

some kind, supplied by the hotel and a manual latch or level latch. With this type of locking you really have the best of both worlds. An easy modern style locking mechanism supplied and controlled by the hotel plus something mechanical and strong that you can use to add additional security. With this type of locking someone with a hotel master key cannot gain entry easily into your room if you are in and have activated both locks. This is about as good as it will get in a hotel.

Remember though the golden rule in a hotel is to assume that a number of people have access to your room. Don't assume you are always safe and secure there. It's a difficult mental concept to maintain as after a few days we start to slip into the subconscious feeling of belonging there. This can lead you to start dropping your defences and forgetting the simple fact that unlike your home there will be a lot of people that may or can have access to your room.

Your security is closely linked to your situational awareness and maintaining that when you feel comfortable sanctuary somewhere especially when under a number of other external pressures such as work, tiredness, travel and general stress is very difficult.

No one wants to be laying in a hotel room scared to go to sleep and the instances of trouble in major brand chains is actually extremely low especially if you consider the sheer numbers of people passing through. However as in everything we talk about it's just a matter of risk management. Stack the odds in your favour, take a few simple precautions and you are more than likely going to remain secure and safe.

Approaching your room regularly gives you the ability, if alert, to recognise that something has changed, different or out of place and that could be the alarm bell you need. However the opposite is true in that you may relax too early feeling that you have reached the sanctuary of your room, your own personal space.

If you have a room with an old manual key then one of the things that sometimes works depending on the type of lock you have is to fully insert your own key from the inside. This way when someone tries to enter from outside using a copied or master key they may not be able to fully insert their key making it useless.

Once inside and having secured the entry into your room then make sure you take precautions when you open the door. Most hotel rooms have a spy hole in the door or some more modern rooms have a camera overlooking the door. Use these security features the hotel has provided, don't just open the door and assume its room service or the evening turn down service.

If you have a latch or chain then use that as you open the door to double check who is outside your room. It's very easy for a person to step right up to the spyhole so that you can't see around or behind them. If they do this it's easy to make it look like there is only one person at the door when there might actually be 2 or more.

The hotel safe or is that a misnomer

So you arrive at the hotel either on business or a holiday and the 1st thing you want to do is safely stash away your passport, spare cash and spare credit card (you do have one of those right?). Most of the time hotels now provide a safe in the room and there is generally two clear chains of thought from travellers. They are either completely secure or the opposite approach of the no way would I trust my valuables to that.

Both approaches have their downfalls, who realistically wants to take all their credit cards and cash to the beach, bar, sauna or gym with them.

So we decide that probably the safe is more secure but as sensible travellers not too jet lagged lets first understand and evaluate the risk. Safety and security is all about identifying, evaluating and understanding risk and then taking suitable action.

There are a couple of considerations before we decide how secure and how much trust we place in the safe

Is the safe placed on a cupboard shelf or is it securely fixed to a solid wall or floor. If you can pick it up and carry it away then it really doesn't matter how good the lock is.

What is the hotel like, all safes have either an override or master key. No hotel would rely on every guest always remembering their combination or in the case of swipe cards not losing that card. So at the end of the day the security of the safe relies on the hotel staff not coming along entering the master code and removing what they want.

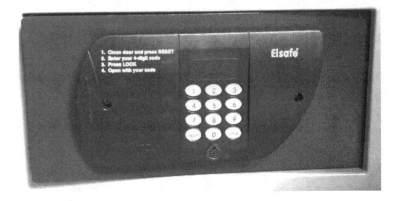

In the picture above you can see a small data connection point on the front of the safe, that's not there for you to use.

Can you spread your risk safely? Safety, security and peace of mind are all about understanding the risks involved and then planning around those risks. If we feel comfortable that by putting things in the safe we can feel OK about walking to that meeting tonight then it has achieved the goals that you wanted.

If you are on business and you feel that the biggest risk is the loss of your passport due to the nature of the country you are in then get a 2nd passport. Not many people realise that you can legally obtain a 2nd British passport. The main difference in the application is you need a supporting letter from your company. When I used to send staff across to some parts of Africa they all had 2nd passports.

So overall is the hotel safe secure - no it's absolutely not.

Is it more secure than carrying your treasures around with you - probably yes?

If you spread your risk between the two options are you increasing the likelihood of completing your trip and returning home safely - **ABSOLUTELY**

Alternative Styles of Safe

When we stayed at the Waldorf Astoria in New York some years ago they were still using lockable safes near the reception area but I'm not sure if this remains the case. There will undoubtedly be hotels that will continue to do this however and where they offer a dual key function these are extremely secure.

Elevators (Lifts)

Stairways and Elevators have advantages and disadvantages. Basically an elevator is a box. In fact it's a box with a restricted entrance and exit that will only open under certain circumstances.

You need to reach a new floor and then press the button to open a door it won't open otherwise. As such if you are in the elevator with someone else you need to realise that any avenue of escape doesn't exist. So if you are in elevator with another person you need to keep all of your senses on alert.

Worse still is most elevators have solid doors so as you approach a new floor the door will open and you have no idea and no warning who is on the other side of that door. As it's the only way in or out you are literally trapped by someone you haven't had the opportunity to evaluate.

Imagine two worse case scenarios.

In the first scenario you are in the elevator of a large hotel on the way down before you leave for the office. Your new Rolex you brought after that last sales bonus is making you feel great, you have your passport and wallet in your breast pocket as you are flying out after the meeting. Life's good, things are going great and you feel like you have finally made it after years of grind and hustle. As the metal door opens on the third floor two men in suits get into the elevator, and you move aside to make sure they can get in easily. Strangely one of the men presses the button for the second floor, oh well they are probably just meeting a colleague you have plenty of time so it's no problem. You turn away quickly as a fist hits your nose and you feel immense pain as the bones break and your front teeth are smashed. You barely notice as one of the men stamps on your head having fallen to the floor. You don't even comprehend what's happening as he takes your watch, wallet and passport. As they get out on the second floor one of the men puts a pen in the doorjamb so it can't shut delaying any help you might have got if the lift were to arrive at reception.

In the second scenario you are a very successful lady having worked your way up to running a large department with over two hundred staff. You have had a great day visiting this office and just need to get back to your hotel room and crash with some room service. As you get in the elevator a young man enters and stands by the door paying you no attention. As the doors open at his floor instead of stepping out he blocks the doorway and three other men enter pushing you against the back wall. With the door held open you are at the mercy of the men in the lift. With the knife at your throat you can't scream for help and are completely trapped.

Both scenarios show how difficult it would be to protect yourself. Anyone who believes they can fight off four attackers is either deluded or an expert.

There are methods of doing so but to say its easy is immensely misleading but we will share the basic principle just so you can picture it in your mind. The principle is to fight only one person at a time, you do this by where you position yourself and if you don't act decisively and quickly they will move to negate this action. Sounds fairly easy doesn't it. Well if you think so go to an elevator with a couple of friends and do it in a light-hearted manner. Maybe give them all a marker pen and see if they can mark your shirt. Yes you guessed right the marker is just a substitute for a knife and the marks are your blood.

If you tried that you will realise how difficult that particular situation is.

Defence in an elevator is difficult to say the least but sometimes life happens and you are in an elevator and just want to minimise your risk. You have 2 basic options on where to stand to help you at least stand a chance and I was debating these with another self-defence instructor. Neither is right or wrong and it is very dependent on each situation.

The first option is to stand well away from the door in the corner of the back of the elevator. This gives you time to react to anyone entering the elevator and by being in the corner you limit the space they have to approach you. Normally corners are considered as places which limit you as you are trapped by the two walls but in this scenario you are trapped anyway. The downside to this approach is it guarantees that you accept the inevitability of the confrontation so you best be able to look after yourself.

The second option is to stand by the side of the door. The partial corner by the side of the door often has the door controls so you have the option of pressing the alarm as well as possibly being able to push your way out and escape before any attackers get the opportunity to size you up and decide whether you are their next victim or not.

Neither approach is fool proof and success depends as much on how your possible attacker plans and initiates any robbery or attack however these are the two possible options. Any other position really puts you at significant disadvantage.

Stairways

The biggest problem with most stairways is that no one uses them.

In most hotels and even businesses the stairways are often tucked away around a corner and sometimes purely treated as a fire escape.

It's a reflection on how people's habits have become more sedentary over the years but unfortunately if you take the stairs you may be one of only a handful that whole day. This means that the chances of

there being safety in numbers is much reduced with little likelihood of you being rescued.

The invention of CCTV has helped but next time you are in a hotel check where the CCTV is pointed as often the stairway cameras only point at the doorways catching people as they enter or leave the stairways. With a hat on and a coat pulled up it's easy for someone to enter the stairs without ever being caught on camera.

Not all stairs and elevators are separated and in this scenario you are advised to take the stairs where possible. Recently I stayed at a hotel where the glass elevator went up the middle of a spiral staircase. In this situation both would be fairly secure but this isn't a common situation. However once again the elevator and stairs didn't have any CCTV, the cameras were simply pointing at the entry door to the stairwell on the ground floor.

The biggest advantage of using stairs is that you can normally see what's ahead and behind you so if you feel you are being followed you have the option to speed up or at least prepare for confrontation with some notice.

The best defence is to run and create as much noise and commotion as possible.

A night out

Many business trip involve evenings out either entertaining guests or simply on your own. What business traveller hasn't sat in a restaurant on their own eating an evening meal?

Please remember that as a businessman or indeed a tourist you may have or appear to have everything that some people don't but think they deserve.

In some countries or indeed areas of major cities or towns it's like having a flag on your head saying you're a millionaire please come and take whatever you want.

If that's a complete mistake it's irrelevant. It's irrelevant that this is your first business trip and you borrowed the money from your parents for the new suit. No one who is following you knows that, to them you look like a rich businessman you may as well have just earned a 100k bonus.

It's not just your property that they might want however, remember jealousy has fuelled many an assault. Maybe the guy following you identifies you as a rich banker and yes he watches the news and as a result hates bankers. It doesn't matter if that's a valid judgement or not it's their belief and that's all that matters to them at the moment they knock you to the floor and use your head as a football.

As a woman in some countries you are statistically less likely to be assaulted in this way although as society changes I predict that those statistics will start to level out. However in some areas if you are out alone at night then it must be fair to assume you are sexually available. Again it doesn't matter if that is right or wrong, the accuracy or reasoning behind that debate are irrelevant. As long as someone believes it and is willing to act on it that's all that matters. You are not trying to educate someone's reasoning you are attempting to stay safe.

Understanding that the reality of an issue is completely irrelevant is a difficult concept but it's one you must embrace. Perception is everything. If someone believes you are rich and they attack you in order to take something it might be worse if you actually don't have anything.

The business drinks

After meeting drinks can be great ice breakers and can be seen as good for the team dynamic.

I have been in many companies where meeting after work or after a project delivers, a new contract is won or a bonus is awarded requires a celebration drink.

Now as in most situations everything is fine and in reality there are millions of these meetings going on around the world every single day. So the statistical likelihood of anything going wrong is again very small.

However there is a reason we aren't allowed to drink and drive. It affects your judgement. What may otherwise seem a stupid or reckless decision suddenly seems fine. You can handle it no problem.

Remember that once you have had a few too many, the likely hood of you realising that and making a well thought out decision on how to avoid further issues is unlikely. Once again we come back to planning. So before you set off, work out how you are getting back, don't leave it until you are very happy with champagne to attempt to work it out.

For those drinking in crowded places that you are unfamiliar with remember the drink aware campaigns that ran a couple of years ago. These campaigns highlighted the issue of someone adding something to your drink.

Assume these warnings were only for single young females out partying and you make the mistake of risking your life. They apply to everyone regardless of status, occupation, sex or position.

There are many drugs that when added to a drink leave you either laid out completely or have a slightly less toxic effect.

These are sometimes known as date rape drugs but experts prefer the designation drug-facilitated sexual assault, but in fact they don't only lead to sexual assaults and definitely not just sexual assaults on young women.

Alcohol in itself could be considered such a drug and you should remember that but in this instance we are looking at possible added drugs which leave the person subdued in some manner.

These could be a vast array of substances so don't assume that these drugs are not readily available. Rohypnol, GHB and ketamine are probably the most commonly discussed but other drugs used include hypnotics such as zopiclone or the widely available zolpidem (Ambien), sedatives such as neuroleptics (anti-psychotics), chloral hydrate or some histamine H1 antagonists, commonly found recreational drugs such as ethanol, marijuana, cocaine, and less common anticholinergics, barbiturates and opioids.

The time it takes for the drugs to take effect differs and so does the time they remain active. Rohypnol for example takes about 30 minutes to take effect whereas Ketamine is very fast acting. Depending on the drug and the amount used you might seem drunk which is why people sometimes don't come to your aid, especially when the person (that kind stranger, but you are now compromised and unable to tell anyone you don't know them) holding and assisting you says don't worry they will look after you and get you home or back to your hotel.

Alternatively the immediate impact can be much stronger and you could become unconscious. Additionally after the drugs have worn off you could experience memory problems being unable to recall either partially or exactly what happened to you and when.

These drugs can leave you in a state that leaves you unprotected for a huge range of crimes from pickpocketing, cashpoint theft, through kidnapping to rape. Total collapse may not be the desired effect from the attacker. They may prefer a state of relaxed compliance so that suspicion isn't raised if staff at the venue are not involved.

Drugs like this can be easily added to drinks by either the bar staff or someone tampering with a drink especially after a couple of alcoholic drinks have had their effect so you don't notice.

Open topped drinks are a significant risk area especially when left while you go to the toilet, dancefloor or leave them unattended in any other way. So for instance draft beer in a glass or a glass of wine are easy targets.

A bottled beer is easier to protect, can easily be carried with you and is less likely to be tampered with prior to being served.

As with many assaults splitting the heard is the method of many assailants. So if out for a drink with colleagues in the evening be additionally alert if you are separated from the group. Once no longer part of the group you are potentially a future victim.

Simple tips to avoid issues

- Open drinks yourself and make sure they are sealed beforehand.
- Don't accept drinks from other people
- Stay with colleagues at all times
- Keep your drink with you at all times
- Don't share drinks
- Don't party on punchbowls or group drinks
- If someone you don't trust completely offers to get you a drink go with them
- If something tastes salty, very sweet or smells strange then avoid it

Remember our overriding golden rule we state again and again.

Nothing is worth more than your health and life. Would you trade your life for the cost of a drink? Simply pour any unknown drink away and get a fresh one.

The Café

The café or bar is a prime location for pickpockets. As people sit and chat, relax over a coffee, beer or glass of wine it's a great chance to go through coat pockets and bags without them realising. If you go to the toilet make sure you take everything with you or when you come back out it might no longer be there.

Remember if the pickpocket didn't know where your wallet or purse was they will as soon as you take it out to pay. Not only that but they may also get a glimpse of how much cash and what cards you are carrying. If your pocket or bag had a clasp or zip in it you have also just demonstrated how to open it and it's then a simple matter of following you outside and helping themselves.

When on a holiday in Mauritius we were sitting at a table outside a restaurant and I had a small backpack. Actually I don't think it had anything of value in at all and if so it would have been very minimal. Anyway I had the backpack by the side of me so had wrapped the strap around my leg. Just then the owner came out and pointed to a guy at the end of the street and said to keep a tight hold of my bag as they would run past the tables outside the restaurants grabbing any bags that they could as they went past. This shows two things, the first was that I had already anchored my bag and the second that the owner of the premises cared about his customers.

This does however raise the question of should I have anchored my bag at all as it was comparatively worthless. I did it out of habit, had I thought logically about it I probably wouldn't have as it certainly wouldn't have been worth fighting over.

I like all of us have learned habits because of what I do and some of these habits are not good habits.

Remember our golden rule nothing is worth fighting over not a bag, car, watch or anything other than your life or that of a loved one. Let it go live another day and claim the insurance.

Looking after your partner or colleague

One of the questions I am asked a lot is how to look after your partner. Now this actually raises a number of questions, firstly why do you think they need looking after, are you overconfident yourself and as a result at more risk that your partner. Maybe your partner should be looking after you.

Overconfidence is a huge problem in self-protection and self-defence. We see it all the time in the academy with big guys who pump iron in the gym assuming that will help them fight. Time and again we end up watching them getting really frustrated when some little guy or girl weighing half what they do, choke them out or punch them at will. What has made it worse is the rise in personal trainers doing pad work with their gym clients, well sorry but most of these gym trainers shouldn't be allowed anywhere near the pads they know worse than nothing. Couple that with some of the heavy iron gyms putting up punch bags and the big guys slugging it suddenly think they can box.

I guess it's a macho thing as we rarely get ladies coming in with the expectation that they will be able to hit the pads well or beat the guys that have been training years. So before you ask about looking after your partner make sure you think of yourself as well. Remember the safety briefing in an airplane, when they discuss the loss of oxygen in the cabin what they say to do first is to put your own mask on so you can help others. The same works for self-protection.

You having being shot or stabbed leaves you in a poor position to be able to look after your partner. Having said all that hopefully we have set a context for your own safety and brought your ego back down to the ground.

Looking after your partner very much depends on context. One of the main areas that I get asked about however is when out shopping or walking along the road.

When out shopping at malls or markets especially where a large number of traders and other people can approach you and your partner I prefer to be slightly behind my partner on one shoulder about arm's length away. This way I am close enough to prevent someone stepping between us, splitting us, but far enough away that I can see people approach from all 4 points of the compass.

Remember our golden rule though. There is little point in your being there if someone were to grab your partners bag and run with you giving chase as you then leave your partner completely alone and unprotected. What someone might steal is irrelevant in protecting your partner. The approach to your partner was when you should have reacted because at that point you were not aware of their intentions. It may have been as was the case to grab their bag it might have been to attack them for their possessions or because of who or where they are. Who knows what the intentions were and that's exactly why you should have intervened if you felt that they were at significant risk.

Often just steering your partner away is enough and they will go and find an easier target. If it was a significant threat in a dangerous risky area then your actions need to match the level of threat.

If you are forced to fight to defend you and your partner you should have made sure you discussed this beforehand. There are huge issues with your partner not knowing what to do in this type of situation.

The last thing you want is for you to leap into action, knock someone to the floor and your partner to pull you off not realising that they have just joined in on the side of your attacker. What if your decision was to run but they misunderstood or reacted differently and instead stayed and started to fight back. Communicate beforehand and at least have a basic understanding.

Catching a cab

The safest place to catch a cab from is the hotel. They often have arrangements with approved companies and recognised drivers.

If the hotel simply calls a cab for you it's still probably safer than if you hail one from the street.

Anyone who has travelled will know that often once you step into the cab the meter miraculously suddenly stops working and you then have to negotiate the price of the journey with the driver.

At this point you have 3 main options

1. Get out of the cab

If at the hotel its fine and the doorman will normally take over the argument for you. If you happen to have left the hotel you have probably stopped somewhere you wouldn't want to get out, that was all part of the con. Identify the risk, evaluate it and make your decision. Don't be too confident and step out into a dangerous area, get mugged raped or killed for what is probably a few pounds.

2. Negotiate the price

Although none of us like feeling ripped off this may well be your safest option. A few extra pounds in exchange for your security and also the ease of simply paying rather than getting out and trying to find another cab may be worth it.

A simple trick for this negotiation is to find out what the rate should be before you hail a cab. If they then want to negotiate at least you know what you should be paying. It can often swing the negotiation considerably if you actually know what the rate should be and you say you have been there many times before.

I remember getting out of a cab in Bangkok after failing to negotiate a reasonable rate following instant meter failure. Fortunately I know the city quite well so felt comfortable with my choice. After hailing another cab and agreeing we would use the meter, in itself quite a surprise in Bangkok, we were waiting at the traffic lights about two minutes from the hotel which was a left turn and the driver had his right indicator on.

I was about to do the twice around the block route before you get to the hotel trick. When I said the hotel was on the left and how to get there the cabbie was most disappointed.

If you open a wallet bulging with high value notes don't expect to get a good price when you negotiate. Have a bit of decency as well as sense don't rub someone's nose in the fact you have loads of cash on you. Have a few small notes to about twice the value of the journey to hand and then start negotiating.

Remember however our guiding principle how much would you pay for your safety and security, a lot more I'm sure than the cabbie is asking. Be realistic as well. If they picked you up from the best hotel in town they know an extra dollar isn't going to hurt you.

3. Insist the meter be used

This may or may not be taken seriously by the driver but in some countries you will have little chance of this.

The theory is sound but only in the context of a cab in a major city such as London, Frankfurt or New York. If you are in any cities in Asia, Africa or South America your ignorance will I'm sure be a source of great amusement to the cab driver.

You may get a few shrugs and a sudden lack of understanding of your language on the part of the cabbie but that's about as much progress as you are going to make.

Time to swap to one of the above two options.

Being Followed

So you believe or suspect someone is following you. Now this could just be that you are unfamiliar with the area, you didn't like the look of the group of men stood at the corner in their hoodies or you just watched a horror movie. It doesn't matter why just trust your instincts.

If you were wrong and no one was following you what is there to loose. Maybe an extra 10 minutes of your time, who wouldn't swap 10 minutes for being attacked. It's like the question on possessions, if asked the question on what you would choose in the cold light of day it's a no brainer however because we feel nervous, silly, embarrassed, belittled it can be easy to ignore the warnings and make the wrong choice.

Nature has given us strong instincts and most people in a modern western world spend their whole lives fighting to supress these instincts so that they fit in. Most of the time there is nothing wrong with that but when the hairs on the back of your neck stand on end or you suddenly feel panicked act on it, take a preventative action to nullify the threat. Trust your feelings and act.

If it means you walk straight into a shop and ask them to call you a cab then what's wrong with that. If you feel embarrassed just say you don't feel too well and most shops will help you.

Remember the rule though, if you didn't make the shop and someone does try to mug you if your life isn't threatened give up your possessions, don't fight and die for something of such little value as a watch, wallet or purse.

Run

Any time you feel threatened or attacked and you feel you can run for it then run.

We have adrenaline for a reason and the fight or flight instinct is a strong one. If you panic and think you can run then run. If attacked run, and I don't mean jog I mean run, run like Usain Bolt in the 100meter finals, run like you have never run before. Run straight into the nearest shop, office or anywhere you think people will be.

When you watch the soaps or thriller on the TV the person being chased always runs straight down the middle of the road even if it's a car that's chasing them. I wouldn't recommend that as the best approach. No you will find me running into a shop, office or creating as much noise and havoc as possible. If it's a residential street I'm not going to knock on a door for help I'm going to be throwing dustbins through windows creating havoc and as much noise and commotion as possible. I will happily pay for a dozen windows if it means I'm alive but well at the end of it.

.

People's fear of feeling stupid

So you were wrong you weren't being threatened and everyone watching you now thinks you are a few bricks short of a full load. So what. Who cares? These are people you will probably never see again. You are safe, you will be able to kiss your partner and children goodnight once again what else matters.

This kind of breaking with the norms of society to ensure your safety is paramount if you are to survive should you be the unlucky one. It really doesn't matter that bystanders may look at you a bit strangely, you should be creating enough noise and commotion that they feel that they can't turn their back and walk away. Don't just shout for help single someone out and point at them ask them specifically to help you. Make people come to your aid, make your attacker run.

For anyone thinking that the people around them will voluntarily come to their aid if they think it's required then you need to think again. There have been a number of recent social studies on this topic some of which have been aired on social media for all to see.

In some cases people will step in but don't forget they are also putting themselves at potentially significant risk. People mind their own business a lot of the time but sometimes they will stand up when needed.

I know of a case for example on a busy commuter train where a lady asked a man if he could stop talking about his sex life so loudly on his mobile phone. The reaction was to threaten her with physical assault in an aggressive way. Fortunately for the lady involved a number of other commuters stood and offered aid and support so the incident rapidly dissolved. To do this is very courageous as those people didn't know if they were taking a huge risk. This unfortunately is not always the case but where it is and an incident is prevented we can all feel much better about the society we live in.

I know for sure that I would want someone to step in to help my family if they were threatened or attacked so it is only fair to assume I should do the same. However as we mentioned before nothing we do is without risk. If you step into a situation without care for your own safety it's possible that it will be you that ends up as the victim.

Public Transport

Public transport is a fantastic opportunity for pickpockets and thieves. It can also be an opportunity for someone looking to commit a serious crime against you or your loved ones.

The biggest change in recent years is the increase in CCTV on public transport. That has helped you the innocent traveller considerably. However don't assume that CCTV means safety.

The London underground is an incredible network and one of the most complex in any city in the world. If you wander around the network you will see CCTV everywhere and that coupled with the surveillance you can't see does provide significant assistance to

the police who patrol.

However don't assume that the pickpockets, thieves and violent drunk don't also know about the CCTV. It's not a secret, deliberately so in order to deter.

As with all instances the tip is to keep valuables safe and not on show so if you are holding the overhead rail and showing the 50 people in your carriage your gold Rolex you probably haven't understood the book so far. I know that sounds a bit farfetched but I have seen it with my own eyes on a packed underground train. They may just as well have hung a sign around their neck saying

I'm rich and a bit careless with my belongings so help yourself.

Massed crowds crushing together in close proximity are a pickpocket's view of heaven. If you really think you will notice your wallet and passport disappearing and being passed from one of the pickpocket team to another you are really misguided.

If we think about our security. Spatial awareness and a recognition of the people and layout of structures around us are vital.

Where you stand or sit on a less busy journey is an essential element of your security. If you sit with your back to the rest of the carriage how will you know if you are at risk if you can't see who is behind you.

If you sit with your back to the wall near an exit or door but not with the door straight in front of it.

If you are near an exit you can make a decision on whether to stay on the train or get off. You get a chance to evaluate risks and make a decision although not perfect it is better than other options.

If you sit or stand directly in front of the exit then anyone standing there or getting on doesn't give you the necessary time to recognise and evaluate the risks. So for example just as the automatic doors close they grab your bag and jump off.

Much more seriously they grab you and jump off, you are now outside the train with your aggressor with no notice.

A similar incident happened to me when I was travelling with my wife on the Milan underground. Fortunately although at the end of a long day my senses were still alert enough to recognise the threat, evaluate the risks and options and to prevent any problems. Remember all of this happens in a second or two and comes from years of planning and role playing and drills to recognise this type of incident and how to react.

By reading this hopefully it's enough to trigger that realisation in you, should you find yourself in a similar situation.

The underground train in question had rows of seats and then glass panels around the section by the train doors. We were stood with our backs to the glass panels about six feet from the doors when three men got on the carriage.

While casually chatting to each other they manoeuvred themselves in a way that intruded on our personal space and attempted to split me from my wife just as we entered the next station. Their plan was quite clearly to push me off the train just before the doors close leaving my wife alone on the train with the three men. I would have been completely unable to help in anyway as I was left standing on the platform as the train departed.

Fortunately as I mentioned I was alert enough to ensure the incident dissolved without this happening.

Situational awareness and simply being prepared and realising that not everyone is as nice as you is absolutely critical in not being caught like this.

One hopes that in this type of situation these people are professional thieves who want as little attention drawn to them as possible because at the end of the day it's bad for business.

If the opposite is true and the people happen to be in it for the thrill of the violence then your actions in dissolving this type of immediate threat is also the early trigger for the violence and you must assume that this is about to occur. If it doesn't then great but don't relax until the threat is absolutely no longer present.

Steaming

Steaming is a form of robbery normally associated with public transport although some similar instances have been referred to as steaming in large crowds such as festivals.

In 2004 five members of a London gang were given a total of 25 years in jail for this type of activity.

Usually this type of attack consists of a large group who all invade a train or bus at one time often using extreme violence to rob anyone on board. The violence is in itself can be the aim with the robbery that goes along with it being seen as a reward for the gang getting their "kicks" from extreme violence.

In the UK, where you cannot carry firearms, your chances of preventing yourself being attacked in this way if unfortunate enough to be on board are minimal. In this sort of instance your goal is to take as little damage as possible. Use any coats or bags you have as a shield and give up your possessions to help ensure as little physical damage to yourself as possible.

You must realise that if there is a large gang intent on this type of attack you are in a serious life threatening situation, no one can stand against a large gang like this unarmed.

Fortunately instances like this are rare and most violent robberies will be undertaken by small groups or possibly individual thieves.

I recently watched a video someone had posted on the internet of a robbery taking place on a bus although the same scenario would apply to any transport.

The bus seated approximately 30 people but was about half full with a mix of people of all ages, race and sizes. Two robbers got on the bus with one pulling a gun at the door and the other with a knife walked up the length of the bus robbing people as he went. One male passenger who was seated fought back as his bag was taken but instead of going 100% at the robber he was half fighting for his bag and shouting he didn't attack the robber and overwhelm him.

As a result the robber stabbed him a few times in the neck and chest and the man slumped back in his seat. To demonstrate that once you are down doesn't mean you will be left alone the robber then went back and stabbed him a few more times even though he was slumped down and unable to move.

Now if we look at this from a self-protection point of view whatever that unfortunate man had in his bag wasn't worth his life. He made a second mistake in that once he decided to fight he didn't give it 100%. Now in his defence he was obviously not trained in any way and was just trying to protect his belongings that were important to him. There was no way to know that his attacker would not only retaliate but would come back and make sure he paid the price for putting up resistance. I am sure that there are hundreds of such videos on the internet and probably as many where the person being robbed manages to fight off an attacker but I use this just as an example of how things can go wrong.

Throughout our guidance has been very clear. DO NOT FIGHT FOR YOUR BELONGINGS THEY ARE NOT WORTH YOUR LIFE. If you do fight either through fear, instinct or the calculation that this is your best chance of survival go 100% with everything you have. Use anything as a weapon. Grab their weapon with all of your strength and head-butt, bite, elbow, claw whatever it takes to come out alive. Anything less and you will probably not make it home.

Prevention is far better than trying to recover from an attack. When boarding a train or bus look at the basic design around you not necessarily where the next free seat is.

If possible sit facing the door, close enough that you might be able to push someone aside and make a run for it but not too close so that as the doors open any attacker is directly and immediately in front of you. Much public transport is under CCTV but this won't necessarily help you in the event of an attack, it may just help Police solve the case afterwards.

Many trains and busses have natural break areas often created by sheets of toughened glass around the exits. These primarily are designed as safety features to break up the tube shaped vehicle you are sitting in in the case of an accident or crash.

Consider how these could shield you if attacked but avoid positioning yourself where they could simply trap you. Your chances of breaking one of these sheets of glass in the case of a serious incident is minimal. In most cases the glass may as well be a see through sheet of steel that you won't be able to get through.

Stay alert on public transport and don't fall asleep as you then have no chance to react should something serious start to happen.

The Car

Running ladies self-defence classes one of the first things we teach them about the car is how to get in and out of the vehicle. Well that seems about as basic and obvious as ABC, how many years have they already been doing this simple task. I think we all know how to get in and out of a car. Well that's true but you don't all know how to do it in a way that provides you with the safest method.

So hands up who opens the door holds the steering wheel puts one leg in sits down and then swings the other leg in and then closes the door. On getting out the reverse is also done.

Now let's think about that for a moment, who amongst us is good at fighting off an attacker, then let's ask again who is good at fighting off an attacker while standing on one leg. I guess it's a few less than ideal. Well think about it for a minute as that's what you are planning on doing, and that's without the attacker slamming the door on your leg that is half in, half out of the car.

Now instead of adopting this method adopt the method where you sit first then swing both legs in together as you close the door. Anytime someone comes up you are now sitting with both legs able to fend off a possible attack. That's a much stronger and more effective method yet equally as simple.

On getting out of the car simply do the reverse, open the door swing both legs out and then use the steering wheel to help you to your feet.

Driving

Why does the fact that you are in a car driving suddenly make you an aggressive assertive person. Road rage as its known is the extreme result of this reaction but much lower on the scale is a lot of anger and aggression before we get to full blown road rage.

Think it through rationally, just let the person move in front of you who is trying to cut in. Yes they are an idiot and yes they should have pulled in behind you but to avoid confrontation simply let them in.

Flip someone the finger because they are driving like an idiot and maybe you will get some satisfaction without any come back but maybe just this one time you did it to the wrong person. The guy on drugs or simply the office worker who has been bullied all day at work and is as mad as hell. What's to stop them cutting in front of you coming back to your vehicle, smashing your window opening the door and dragging you out. Think it hasn't happened? Check the news archives and you will see it has.

Worse still they may not seek immediate retribution they could simply follow you and get even at a later date either with you or your family. Why would you bring this type of trouble to your own door?

Remember the vehicle you are in is a little metal box but it's not a box without any come back. Many people feel invincible while in the vehicle and grow a huge level of bravado that they really don't deserve to carry around with them. It's not who they are. The metal box has changed them into some tough gangster but really they aren't like that at all they are simply an office worker who hasn't had a fight in the last 30 years. If you make the mistake of believing in your false reality that you have just created then it's possible you could pay for that with your life.

Let's assume that you didn't make the mistake of aggressive driving, you were just not looking very carefully and didn't see the vehicle coming from the side who had to break suddenly to avoid you. That person also happened to be the real angry guy and wants a piece of you in retribution for daring to spoil his ego.

Now is the time to remember that you are in a metal box. It's not an unbreakable box but nonetheless it's still a metal box. I'd rather be in my vehicle if someone walks over to try and assault me than standing at a bus stop on the street. At this point remember there is no need for you to answer any confrontation and at no point under any circumstances should you get out to argue with them. Don't wind your window down, don't open your door, check your locks and act as soon as possible and If possible drive away. If you aren't blocked in on all sides by traffic there is no reason you can't simply drive away.

Don't let your pride and ego kill you, just drive away safely. If you have to apologise then do so but if you do apologise don't compromise your situation to do so just in case that apology isn't accepted. Sometimes you can deflate people's aggression simply by showing the opposite. If you can apologise and walk away without appearing week then you have truly mastered the art of body control and this leaves you in a very strong position.

I remember being in my vehicle with my family when I upset someone in a carpark. I can't remember who was at fault but really at that stage it's irrelevant anyway. I was some distance from them and had a clear view of their whole vehicle and everyone in it. Anyway the other driver who looked mad as hell got out of his vehicle and started to approach mine.

Now bear in mind I had my family with me as well so my safety radar was on full alert. If needed yes I am slightly different to many and yes I could fight and hopefully take him down but what if it all went wrong how does that leave my family, not only witnessing my trouble but at a huge risk.

I had plenty of visuals around and space and distance to drive away if needed so my risk factor was small as long as I remained in the vehicle.

I simply wound my driver's window down and leant out and apologised, this came from a confident position so carried confidence as well as the right words. At this stage the other driver was half way between the 2 vehicles and stopped in his tracks. If he had run up to me I would have driven off leaving him to run back to his vehicle before he could chase us. As it was he muttered something along the lines of "well that's ok then but don't do it again" and slopped off back to his vehicle. Now that's a victory.

If the person seeking to confront or attack you is armed then you must get away, it doesn't matter if they have a hammer, a wheel brace or a knife you must get away. At this point accept the inevitable don't take any chances just get away immediately.

Remember if the person is armed with a firearm the vehicle you are in will not shield you from the bullets if they come your way regardless of what you may have seen in the movies. Assume that if they fire the bullets can pass through the vehicle you are in and possibly as a result pass through you. Swerve the vehicle and create distance as quickly and with as much purpose as you can muster.

It's a hard reality but if an assailant is armed with a knife or firearm then unless you have a very high level of training or you yourself are armed then your chances diminish considerably.

That doesn't mean give up but accept that to disarm an assailant if you are unarmed is extremely difficult. If you have no training and are unarmed then the task becomes almost but not quite impossible.

Several years ago I was sitting on the M25 which is known by many as the London carpark due to the amount of traffic jams. Sitting in the outside lane my car hadn't moved for about 10 minutes. I had the radio on and wasn't paying attention to what was going on around me, boredom and frustration had set in. Just then a man in a business suit ran past my window. Now that was not usual not on a parked motorway, and when I say ran past he was going for it, just then another man ran past waving a pair of nunchaku, (martial arts weapon) above his head shouting after the first man. I didn't get out and give chase but did call the police who said they were

106

already on their way. I have no idea what caused the confrontation or if that was the cause of the holdup but it does show that violent aggression is around us and can start without much warning at all.

Breaking down

Breaking down just sucks. It never happens when you have lots of free time it always happens on the way to something important, in the rain or at night. Being prepared can be a huge help. I strongly recommend everyone to be a member of one of the breakdown services. Which one is a matter of personal choice, recommendation and cost but make sure their priority is to get you moving again. That's the big ticket item and the one that is likely to mean that you are not stranded without a vehicle for too long. Remember it's advisable not to sit in a broken down car even on the hard shoulder of the motorway as there have been a number of cases of vehicles driving into the back of broken down cars.

An emergency kit in the car is always a good idea. I normally recommend a first aid kit, a spare torch, an emergency tyre inflation bottle, a good wheel brace, a bottle of water, a set of waterproof high visibility clothing and an air pump. That will actually get you out of a lot of small issues.

Remember that while waiting for the break down service you are personally vulnerable. Everyone knows you can't drive away so you should if possible seek a safe haven such as a restaurant or shop. If you are stranded in the middle of nowhere all alone then you need to keep your wits about you and if in a high risk area I would suggest hunkering down and not attracting any attention. If you are in the USA and you carry a firearm make sure as always its ready and you are prepared.

Central locking

For those of us that are old enough to remember, the invention of central locking was a huge improvement. No more leaning across the seats trying to unlock one of the other doors. Additionally once in all doors can be locked from the press of a single button.

The down side of central locking or automatic unlocking with keyless cars is that once the driver's door opens all the doors open. This means that anyone crouching down by the side of one of the passenger doors also has access to the car.

Once in the car simply lock all the doors. If you don't lock the doors then every time you stop at a junction, in traffic or at lights it is perfectly possible for someone to open one of the passenger doors and get into the car with you. Alternatively they may just open the door and steal your bag or laptop.

When we run our self-defence courses one of the games we play is for the person to drive once around the block. We know that they will have to stop at the end of our parking area as it turns onto a main road. Additionally you cannot see around the corner to your passenger side. As the cars stop one of the instructors who is in waiting opens the passenger door. Lesson learnt.

Parking

Parking safely is actually very difficult to accomplish. There are so many ways that where, when and how you park can be used by a possible attacker that unless it's secured parking then most situations contain elements of risk.

Where you park and the setup of the area around where you park is absolutely crucial for your safety.

As you approach the car from a distance you should be able to see underneath without bending or making it difficult. This is another reason that if possible clear visibility of the car from a distance as you approach is advisable. It is possible for someone to be the other side of the car and you not be able to see them if they position themselves by one of the tyres so bear that in mind.

One of the big problems with parking is that you need space between you and your car to assess the situation and decide on what to do. So for example if I have time to look across the road at my car and decide if I should walk away or approach then that's just great. In reality this is actually quite difficult. Other people may be around, you may not feel that secure so you want to get to your car for safety, you may not physically be able to park in the type of position you wish. Maybe all the best spaces are no parking zones.

Time and space to assess and decide what to do are the key, so if your vehicle is parked on a corner then as you walk around that corner the car is immediately there only feet away and it's very difficult then to make an assessment.

If paying at a meter, be aware of who is around you and watching as you show where your money is held

In the two pictures here we have a situation where if you approach your vehicle you can't see around the corner. You have no idea if someone is stood there and won't be able to make any kind of assessment of the threat until you are at the corner giving you no time to prepare to defend yourself or run.

As you can see from the next picture the corner is actually a perfect position for an attack as it leads directly to an alleyway and out to another road giving any potential attacker every opportunity to attack and then make good their escape. If the motive wasn't a simple robbery then they have an escape route should anything go wrong with their plan of attack.

A Similar situation is shown in the following carpark. In the first picture below it doesn't actually at first glance look too bad a position. We have plenty of visual space as we approach the vehicle. However you cannot see the other side of the car so someone could easily be hiding by the tyres on the other side.

That same position viewed from the opposite side shows that an attacker could easily be hiding on the opposite side of the corner waiting for the driver to approach. They would be unseen until the very last second making this a significant risk.

In order to ensure your safety you park along a busy row of parked cars and under a street lamp. Understanding the previous issue of someone waiting nearby the vehicle is across the street from you as you approach so everything seems to be fine and you are happy with your choice of parking spot.

After work when you return to the car you find that everyone else parked on the street has already collected their car and left. Your car is the only one in the street and as you see the vehicle there are groups of men standing nearby. Due to the fact that the only reason you would approach or walk along that part of the street is to collect your car then what should have been the perfectly safe situation now means that you have a clear choice. Approach the vehicle or turn away before anyone sees you. This sort of scenario is why you need to stay alert and be prepared to change your plans if things go a bit pear shaped.

In the above picture you can see that a car parked in the middle of a busy carpark during the rush hour stands out like a beacon as you arrive after everyone else has gone home. Anyone fancy walking to the vehicle all alone with maybe some gangs hanging around.

In general when you approach the car if you get the opportunity have a quick glance at the back seat area just to ensure no one has entered your car and is crouched down behind one of the front seats waiting for you.

Likewise any time you get out of the car lock it. If you go to get fuel or anything like that lock your car.

Don't allow the opportunist to either steal from you or get into the car unnoticed.

After viewing some of the less obvious poor parking choices I hope that no one is now considering using the parking shown above.

Waste ground, broken security gates, no street lighting and no one else parked along the street should be enough of a warning to anyone thinking of gambling on this location.

Car Accident

Accidents happen but you have a couple of situations that you need to take additional care about. The first is the other driver losing their cool as a result of the accident. Maybe that car is their pride and joy that they wanted their whole adult life and you just smashed into the side of it. Uncontrolled anger is a huge issue and you need to be aware that this could be one of the outcomes of any accident. Don't take risks and don't argue or accept liability. If you read most insurance policies it states that you cannot accept liability and if you do then they will not necessarily pay out.

The second type of accident is one that's a scam not a true accident. Here's how it works. You are driving when someone drives in the back of your car. As you get out to inspect the damage someone either in the other car involved or an accomplice waiting nearby attacks you and takes your car keys and steals your car.

If ever you are attacked for your car keys the advice would be to hand over the keys and run away. Hopefully they are too interested in taking your car to chase you as well.

If at all suspicious or travelling alone and you are involved in a minor accident take their registration details and drive to the nearest police station and report the accident.

Alternatively you could stay in your vehicle. Always keep your doors locked if approached and just crack the window enough to swap insurance details.

The whiplash scam

As you slow down or pull up at lights the car in front reverses into you. They can then claim that you actually drove into them and claim insurance compensation for the whiplash.

If this happens to you simply record the details and contact the police. Do not start an argument at the incident unless police are there where you can state what happened. Do not admit guilt as it may be recorded in these days of smartphones simply state what happened and then contact the police and your insurance company. At the end of the day you are safe and you have insurance. The only way of preventing this is to use a dashboard mounted camera.

The Victim Needs Help

There was a scam reportedly running for some time mainly on quieter roads. You are either flagged down by another motorist who is at an accident or you notice someone injured in the road.

As you pull up the casualty or an accomplice either gets in the car with you or drags you out. Either way you have just been carjacked.

It is far better for you if they drag you out and drive off as you are not trapped inside your vehicle. Never under any circumstances try and stop them driving the car away. Why would you risk serious injury by being run down if there is no immediate risk to yourself?

If they take the car and drive off you have achieved your main aim in these types of confrontation, you are safe and away from the attackers. Worry about the car and the insurance later but in the immediate aftermath just act to ensure your immediate safety.

Boxing In

Boxing in can be done on motorways or any other roads. The principle behind boxing in is the same the police use to bring a car to a standstill except in this case its used as an attack on you.

A car will either be in front of you or will overtake and then place themselves in front of you. A second car will then come up from behind and a 3rd car will overtake but sit by the side of you.

Start   **Boxed In**

You are effectively boxed in on 3 sides now and if there is any kind of barrier, fence hedge on the nearside of your vehicle you are boxed in on 4 sides. By all three of the boxing in cars slowing down this tactic can be used to stop your car. If the car on the outside of you starts to move over towards you this tactic can be used to make you turn off or pull into a layby.

If you are caught in this type of scenario it's because you have been targeted. As a result of not being alert or aware that you were at risk you have been caught in an emergency situation completely by surprise.

Once in the situation it's a very difficult one to control, this is the reason the police use this tactic. You have two basic options the first is to slow down as they do so and comply.

The alternative is to slow down and once either stationary or just beforehand attempt to accelerate and escape through a gap between two of the cars. This will undoubtedly lead to a collision and you must be sure that you are prepared for both the collision and any subsequent chase and further attempts to push you off the road.

The choice you make largely depends on why the people have boxed you in. If you don't know why you have to make a judgement call. For instance if you have a very expensive car then it's likely a carjacking or robbery. If it's a carjacking it may be more judicious to simply give up your car and make good your escape. If you are a person of fame rather than fortune then you may be the target of a kidnap attempt.

Confrontation

Assault

We have looked at so many scenarios and confrontations throughout the book but an area that is often missed when discussing business travellers is the actual assault. That moment when everything has gone wrong and physical confrontation at some level, an unknown level at present is going to occur regardless of anything you say or do.

Let's consider this for a moment before we get too carried away with what to do next. I strongly believe that in the majority of cases the assault is as a consequence of failing to do the right things. In saying that lets make it clear it's not our fault that the terrorist plants their bomb or the drug addict needs a fix and cash to pay for that. We can only address the things that we can change worrying about anything else is simply a waste of energy and brain power.

If it's a face to face confrontation that leads to the assault then there are opportunities somewhere in that situation prior to that point where we either had an opportunity to change the other person's perception or actions or where we should have pre-emptively acted maybe by turning right instead of going left. Did we miss or misread the danger signals for instance. This is true self protection and the continued effort to avoid the dangerous situation is our role, that's what we should be attempting continuously. Avoid the situation and then you aren't going to be the victim.

Having said all of that there are inevitably times when we just got it wrong. Maybe after coming off a flight and attending a day of meetings we are a bit distracted, so as we head out of the hotel that evening to go for dinner we fail to recognise the fact someone is following us. It's not our fault that person is waiting outside the biggest business hotel in the city to rob someone but it's our fault we didn't recognise the risks and the situation developing.

Nature did a great job for us though. If you ever watch a nature programme on the TV you will often see the gazelle suddenly pricks its ears up and then runs before they have seen the lion. They are off and moving as their instincts signalled danger before they had time to recognise it and decode what was going on. We have the same instincts but over the years of living in a comfortable modern society these have become dulled and are often laughed at and deliberately ignored.

If the hair on the back of your neck stands up or you just feel like someone is staring at you then trust your instincts. It's highly likely that this reaction which has been developed over thousands of years is warning you. Ignore these instincts at your peril.

I was discussing this with a former Special Forces operative who said that they were actively encouraged to trust these instincts. Even if they couldn't quite work out why they felt strange or what the threat was they were encouraged to recognise that something had triggered their instincts to fire off warning signals.

If physical conflict is inevitable you have a fight or flight instinct, let your body tell you what to do and then commit 100% to that choice.

If you feel threatened you can decide to attack first if you think that is your best chance of survival. The law in each country is different however survival is always the same. If you are truly threatened and believe your life is at risk and feel you have an opportunity to attack then do so. Even the UK law allows this and UK law is notoriously dubious with regards to victim's rights.

Remember if attacked and you decide to run you must commit 100% anything less is suicidal. The same applies if you decide your only option is to fight. Many take the option to run but don't commit to it. That's a huge mistake. If I decide to run then I'm running like the wind, faster than anything you have ever seen before. Don't jog away from a confrontation run like crazy your life could depend on it.

Rape and sexual assault

In having a discussion on sexual assault and rape it's important to remember this type of assault doesn't only apply to women. I know that's how society and the media report it but it applies to men as well. At the moment it's believed to be less likely to apply to men but don't assume just because someone is male then this doesn't apply.

For this book we will assume in general we are discussing an attack on a female but the general information applies to both sexes.

As I mentioned before the rights or wrongs of how you can and should dress as a woman on a night out are irrelevant. The fact that in many western countries it's not just acceptable but a normal everyday occurrence for either sex to dress as they like don't assume that applies across the globe.

Additionally just because you are travelling in the UK, Europe or USA and equal rights are strong and upheld that everyone in those societies feels that is right.

Someone somewhere thinks that because you have a short skirt on or your head uncovered or some other signal that maybe only they identify with then you are sexually available. Is that right, no it isn't but if you ignore this you are putting yourself at possible risk. By all means campaign to change people's opinions, campaign for equal rights but don't ignore the fact that some may have the opposite view to you. Right or wrong don't matter as long as someone has a belief and they are willing to act on it.

The same applies for gay rights, what is acceptable to most people in the UK will land you in jail in some countries. If you ignore the fact that even in the UK there are individuals and groups that remain hostile to people living their lives as they wish you could be significantly increasing your risk of assault. I'm not saying don't live your life as you wish what I am saying is be alert to the people and environment around you.

Please remember that if the absolute worst case happens and you are the victim of a sexual assault and you aren't in your home country contact your embassy or consulate immediately for assistance and support. Unfortunately in some countries you won't be seen as a victim if you report a sexual assault to the police. In some countries you could find you are ignored or find yourself being arrested for having sex outside of marriage.

Don't assume your own cultural measure of your rights and laws applies around the globe it doesn't.

Contact representatives from your own country immediately not the local police and let them help you. Back home you and your family pay taxes now is the time to collect, don't struggle and suffer on your own seek help but from your countries representatives.

Fight Back

Without training the decision to fight is probably not a good one but if you do then everything and anything goes.

It may seem strange that someone who teaches self-defence and martial arts including working with door staff, forces personnel and security contractors who work in some of the world's hotspots is telling you not to fight. Well that's because a little knowledge can be lethal and not to your attacker but to yourself. If you want to learn to fight then start learning as it will take a few years. It's why I personally push self-protection rather than self-defence. Don't get me wrong we can train people and to a level where they are quite competent with a few basic principles but if they come up against someone who is trained either officially or street trained then they will be unlikely to prevail. I feel false confidence is as likely to kill you as any attacker.

Very early on in my training I spent time with a great instructor (Sensei Pat O'Keefe) who was not only very skilled at what he taught but was also a practical martial artist more than capable of teaching self-defence. Many of the public believe that all martial arts instructors can teach self-defence but that's absolutely not true. Self-defence and martial arts are two very different things and some martial arts instructors in my view teach techniques as dangerous to you as they are the attacker.

I remember a lesson a long time ago where he made us all laugh by explaining the implications of KISS.

Keep It Simple Stupid.

It's quite possible that he won't remember that lesson as it was one of thousands he taught but for me it was the time that the penny dropped, one of those moments that changes your perception and approach.

If you do martial arts or believe you can fight back and you have complicated moves and maybe hundreds of them then you may be living under a false sense of security. Simple basic moves which work and follow some basic principles work time and time again.

If someone was going to mug you and then leave you alone and you instead mess up their plan by fighting back its very possible the incident could escalate either deliberately or accidentally to a life threatening situation. Remember the only golden rule we have don't fight for anything other than your life or the lives of your loved ones. No possession is worth your life.

As a word of caution let me start by saying you are at a huge disadvantage even before the fight starts.

Your attacker has been preparing himself for this maybe for hours or even days. They have either singled you out for some reason or another or possibly you were just the first person to walk around that corner at that time. They are psyched and ready, adrenaline is pumping, they could be drugged, drunk and possibly armed, but most significantly they are ready. It's happening now on their terms. They don't care about the consequences, if you try to protect your wallet they might not care if they stab or shoot you in return.

You. You are probably still unaware that it's about to happen. So even if you are trained you are at a disadvantage. If you aren't trained multiply that by a thousand.

Now if you do listen to your instincts and your adrenaline pumps and you turn to fight are you prepared to start a pre-emptive strike or are you concerned about the law and what if you were wrong and they only wanted to ask the time. Your attacker has none of these social ties holding them back. Maybe they have been to jail before maybe they have killed before or maybe they are just desperate for their next drug fix.

So you can see that everything is stacked against you. It's why we do everything we can to prepare people not to be in that position, everything is already against you before you even start to fight.

When running self-defence courses we try and persuade people as much as we can to run or escape. To get to a place of safety which could be anywhere form your car to a shop. It really isn't a good idea to fight unless you have absolutely no choice at all.

If you do fight then strike hard, fast and until you can either run or the person is unable to come after you. Once you decide to fight you have no choice but to go with everything you have. Don't just hit them and annoy them even more you must attack and attack hard with everything and then get away.

We always suggest you go for simple soft areas that are closest to you such as grab a finger and snap it, then hold it and wriggle it until you get a chance to strike more effectively. Use elbows and claw attacks as much as you can.

Learning techniques won't work, learn a couple of principles and utilise them and if possible use a weapon. You need something to try and even up the odds a bit. Everything is a weapon. A chair, umbrella, pen, flashlight are all weapons that can be used to help you.

In the USA depending on the state you live you may have the option of carrying a firearm. You will then need to decide on concealed carry or not, as well as the firearm you pick. My main concern with firearms is the lack of ability of many people who own them. If you live in the USA and a state that allows you to carry firearms and it's a choice you feel comfortable with make sure you get the appropriate training. A huge disadvantage with firearms is that if you don't know what you are doing you are probably as likely to shoot yourself or an innocent passer-by as any attacker.

For most of Europe firearm carry isn't an option and I wouldn't suggest you carry any other weapon. Apart from any legal implications of carrying a weapon it's highly likely that any weapon you have may be taken off you by an attacker and used against you.

Improvised weapons however do help even the odds sometimes. The best self-defence improvised weapons are ones which are legal and are highly unlikely to be used against you. Everything you have is a weapon, use any weapon you have to hand. Umbrellas, bags, pens, flashlights anything can be used as a weapon.

One of the least obvious weapons for self-defence is a rolled up magazine. It's highly unlikely that it can be used against you but it is very effective.

Fight, fight as hard and viciously as you can and make good your escape.

Catastrophic Situations

Disasters that befall us

I sincerely hope that this sort of situation never happens to you or anyone you know. The chances are extremely stacked against you ever coming across a catastrophic situation and I hope that is the case.

For the purposes of this book what I count as catastrophic situations may not be counted as such by many including governments but these are situations I consider are completely beyond your remit and control and that you have absolutely no chance of avoiding or affecting the overall situation.

You can however try and affect the outcome for you as an individual. Either way these events are of a magnitude that they will change your life.

The sorts of situation I am considering here are both natural and manmade and we will skim over most of the situations but hopefully give you a taste of what could occur and how you need to be thinking if you wish to survive.

Natural Disasters

There are obviously lots of natural disasters that can occur and the likelihood of being involved depends partly on where you are in the world but also on your luck that day. We cannot cover all situations or do we need to, as I mentioned earlier techniques don't and won't work at the best of times let alone in these kind of situations. However by covering what we have I hope that we can cover some basic principles and prepare you mentally.

We have included some manmade disasters in this category as although they are not natural they are unintentional and we will use that as our main divider of consequences.

- **Earthquake**
- **Tsunami**
- **Hurricane**
- **Other natural disaster**
- **Some manmade disasters in this category**
  - **Traffic Accident**
  - **Plane crash/shipwreck**

Now if you survive the initial stages of a natural disaster then you have to consider if the other survivors cause you an immediate danger and if the environment poses additional dangers.

So for instance with an earthquake you have to consider further aftershocks, falling buildings and the possibility of other actions such as a Tsunami, flooding or land subsidence such as mud slides.

It's possible also that the natural disaster may not bring out the best spirit in people it could possibly bring out the opposite effect. With the trappings of an ordered society removed are you now at a huge risk of rape or assault from other survivors. This is an awful area of thought as why wouldn't everyone be helpful and work together but unfortunately not everyone is wired the same as me and hopefully you. Maybe this is the opportunity they dreamt of.

If you cast your mind back to two recent natural disasters you see two very different situations.

The Tsunami that hit Thailand and a lot of Asia in December 2004 devastated whole communities and towns yet overall there were reports of survivors pulling together to help overcome the huge problems and make survival more likely. Local populations worked with travellers and holidaymakers to survive and help with basic needs. For example on some of the Thai Islands travellers who survived stayed behind to help the local population rebuild.

However if we then think of Hurricane Katrina which hit New Orleans USA in 2005 exposed and amplified everything that was wrong with the great city. The huge impact of the hurricane brought out the racial and financial difficulties and the massive differences suffered by the various different populations. Vigilantes and gangs had free reign to operate without immediate legal consequences. It's reported that shootings and rape became significant issues with police either overwhelmed or not present to help for weeks after the initial impact.

In any natural disaster you have 3 priorities

- Ensure your initial survival is reinforced - Beware of follow up problems like a second wave or aftershock.
- Reinforce your safety, make continuous risk assessments and take steps to ensure your continued safety. From both nature, infrastructure and other people.
- Plan longer term survival or escape.

The key to survival following a natural disaster situation is to assess your situation immediately. You must protect your life and your loved ones all alone assuming that the usual benefits and support of a modern society are no longer there.

After you have ensured your immediate survival you must seek out a clean source of water. You can live without food but not without water. If you need to drink unsecured water attempt to boil it first if at all possible as water sources will quickly become contaminated by sewage and other contaminates.

Once you have water your next priority is shelter. Even in warm climates nights can become very cold and you need to protect yourself from wild animals and possibly other people as well.

The 3rd priority is food and then escape and rescue.

Don't assume people will rescue you but prepare for the possibility they will. If there is a huge area affected the area that you are in might not be reached for a while. If you can gather anything to allow signalling then do so. Mirrors, whistles and smoky fires all have uses in this kind of situation. If there are floods and you take to a rooftop then take a bedsheet with you if you can to aid with any signalling.

Man Made

As mentioned above for the purposes of this book we have mixed up the manmade or natural to group them together better by consequences but key manmade catastrophic events are

Terrorist incident

Bomb attacks

Hijacking

Kidnapping

War or Rebellion

Think this doesn't apply to you, let's hope you are right. However with terrorism always an issue somewhere in the world you could unwittingly find yourself in this situation.

Years ago I had a member of staff working in part of Africa and he was there to supposedly strike a deal on new printers for the local government. As he was going to be some days he was staying in a hotel used by foreigners particularly reporters in the capital.

I was in the office when a call came through and I couldn't hear a thing the line was so noisy. I was almost shouting down the phone trying to be heard and I could hear the other person shouting back but not make out what they were saying. Suddenly there was a lull in noise and then lots of interference. This was then followed by the voice of my guy in Africa saying that he was laying under his bed in the hotel and could I let his wife know he was ok as the capital was under attack. The loud noise I had heard was a RPG hitting his hotel. If we had any idea that this would have happened there is no way we would have sent him but it just shows that overnight things can sometimes change beyond all recognition. For those interested he was safely rescued some weeks later perfectly well and unhurt.

Remember all the people who boarded planes in the USA on Sept 11th 2001 and those on the on board the Italian cruise ship Achille Lauro in October 1985. These are two very well-known incidents where ordinary people were going about their everyday business when everything in their world imploded around them.

In these situations the biggest problem is that you aren't an expert. You haven't gone through years of training like the Special Forces, so how do you act and react. Forget everything you see in the movies nothing actually happens like that and if it did the biggest issue, one of pure unadulterated fear doesn't show.

As business people running companies it's hard to imagine how out of your depth you will be. I always try and relate a situation to something we are familiar with but in this case it is difficult to do so. However try to think of it like the first day of work after leaving school but instead of starting as the office junior someone made the mistake of taking you on as CEO. That's how out of your depth you are.

That situation is what you have less than a minute to accept and learn. Put in your usual business situation it sounds a bit more unlikely now that you will survive. It's not like watching a James Bond film and unfortunately the people against you may be very experienced, they could be ex-military or police and you are a complete novice.

Abduction & Kidnap

If it's possible to become anonymous then do so. Unless you have to have your picture and that of your family published then avoid doing so. If for example you are a multi-millionaire or a famous investment banker why on earth would you want your picture spread everywhere? Imagine all the jealous people who can't have what you have, unless of course, they take it from you. There must be lots of people bitter and disappointed with their own failed miserable life so why not take a bit of yours. In their mind why should you have it if they haven't? If you are confident that you are stronger and can stand up to them then what about your wife or children. I know you wouldn't want them being taken and held either out of malice or as hostages for payment.

If you are a person of note then make sure you don't have a routine.

Why make a kidnapper's job easier than you need to. If you do then all you do is increase the number of people who could effectively carry it out. If you are difficult to take then the person who does so is an expert if not then you are saying any fool could do it and there are a lot of fools in the world

The easiest thing you can do is vary your schedule. In fact don't have a schedule. Vary the route you take, vary the time you take it. Park safely and be additionally alert at every transition, so when you step out your house/car/office etc.

Unfortunately compliance does not always lead to survival they are not necessarily directly associated. The passengers on the planes attacked over the USA on Sept 11th were taken as hostage and probably assumed they would be ransomed or traded for prisoners. That in itself is terrifying enough. They would know that their lives were at risk and maybe they wouldn't get a chance to see another day. Previously in the majority of cases the aim of the terrorists was to use passengers as bargaining tools that was what had typically happened previously so why would they possibly even consider they would be flown directly into buildings as makeshift missiles.

Previous experiences had shown that in the majority of instances the best advice is to keep a low profile and blend into the sea of other passengers. Without knowing the full details I would assume that most passengers instinctively took this approach. In most situations that would be the recommended course of action and normally ends with the majority if not all the passengers surviving.

There was the very famous exception of the passengers on United Airline flight 93. After being hijacked several passengers managed to make phone calls and found other hijacked planes had been flown into the twin towers of The World Trade Centre in New York and the Pentagon in Virginia. With this knowledge everything changed and they heroically fought back. It's reportedly not clear from the flight recording recovered if the hijackers fought over the controls with the passengers or if they crashed deliberately before this happened. Unfortunately the plane crashed in Somerset County

Pennsylvania with no survivors. This incident shows how events can change as being cooperative passengers hadn't helped passengers on the other flights that day prompting those on board Flight 93 to attempt to regain control.

At the time of writing the majority of the security advice from different governments recognises that the events of September 11 2001 may result in a change in its guidance in the future but at present the guidance remains to try and cooperate where possible.

Should a hijack occur you need to understand what is likely to happen that way you will be more able to be prepared.

The initial takeover could be very quiet with no incident and just announced by one of the hijackers or crew. Alternatively there could be lots of shouting or possibly shooting.

Remain calm and if there is shooting try to lay down on the floor or at least get your head down

Don't challenge verbally or physically the hijackers

Try to remain calm and attempt to help other passengers remain clam

Beware not all the hijackers may reveal themselves. There could be another hijacker remaining hidden as part of the passengers to either stop any passenger unrest, attempts to retaliate or to draw out any security personnel on the flight such as a sky marshal or intelligence services.

Passengers may be separated according to nationality, race and sex.

Your passport may be taken from you and some passengers may be attacked due to their nationality.

If the aim is a prisoner release or some other demand it's possible that the plane may divert to a different destination and you may be held for some time.

Try to remain calm, avoid any political or racial discussions with anyone and play down your wealth or career. Minimise your importance to the hijacker by keeping answers short, don't give up any information not asked as it may be used against you.

If you travel to Israel and have two passports give up the passport without Israeli immigration stamps. If you are directly confronted confirm your job takes you to Israel and say that you simply use your standard personal documents whenever you travel.

The end of any hijack attempt will be very tense. If the hostages get everything they demanded then there will be massive tension as they stress about the final stages of their hijack.

If security services become involved and attempt a rescue don't take any risks and try to remain clam.

Don't do anything that could confuse you with one of the hijackers. Do as instructed and keep your head down, remember everyone will be under huge pressure including the passengers, rescuers and hijackers and there may be explosions and shooting. Do as told and if instructed to lay down or move quickly then do so.

If you escape as part of any rescue attempt do not be surprised if you are treated as a hijacker until proven otherwise. React calmly and be helpful to the authorities, attempt to request that you be allowed to speak to your embassy or consulate.

Remember you may not have any documentation such as passport or travel documents as they may have been confiscated.

Defensive Driving

The kind of car you drive, where you drive and where you park all influence your risk and vulnerability to kidnapping, assault and car bombing.

As with everything else we have discussed you don't want to stand out from the crowd so if everyone is driving a beat-up old Fiat and you are in a brand new Mercedes you haven't been listening to what I have said so far.

If you are working for a large corporation or a government department you may consider avoiding any branded vehicles or those with special plates.

During the troubles in Northern Ireland it was common for car number plates to be clocked by spotters often referred to as dickers. So if you went to a government building, a strong loyalist area, army or police base it would be known. Maybe if the decision was taken by one of the Republican chiefs the person with that number plate could be paid a visit later on. Maybe in their hotel or even by a car bomb. This type of pattern isn't unique to Ireland and has been used repeatedly in different areas around the world. One of the things with these spotters is they are often young kids working their way into the organisation so your alarm might not be raised.

If you are at threat from car bombing you would normally have been given specialist advice on how to identify if your vehicle has been tampered with. If you haven't then stop what you are doing and go and get expert help immediately. There are experts who have worked extensively in this arena and can give you significant advice. Like everything it's not an absolute defence but it's better than not having any understanding.

The biggest risk is usually outside your home or hotel as this is typically where they know the car will be and where it is parked for the longest period of time. It's also a transition from one environment to another so automatically you are already at a higher risk.

If you are at risk of kidnap remember you should be varying your route and times and avoiding a schedule. This makes the opportunity of taking you in traffic or pulling across in front of you much harder to employ.

If you feel you are being followed then double round the block, if someone recognises that they have been noticed following you that's ok but don't take any action that would provoke them to act there and then. If you are definitely being followed you need to go to a place of safety, this could be your office or embassy or at a push any large public area such as a shopping mall or large hotel.

If your vehicle is under attack in a kidnap attempt you have a choice to make and neither option is desirable. You could either stop, let the inevitable happen or you could try and escape. Whichever option you choose it's unlikely that you would get more than a couple of seconds to make it. This is why risk assessment and planning is so important. If you have done this work beforehand your options have already been played out lots of times in your head, in discussions with advisors or on paper.

If you decide to flee then make noise sound the horn, mount the kerb etc. to escape. Try not to hit the kerb at 90 degrees as you are likely to strip the tyres from the car. However as long as you are moving you are fleeing and once that decision is made nothing is going to stop you. Don't start to flee then change your mind, any decision is a good decision, no decision could be fatal. Stand with your convictions and commit to the choice you made.

If you need to hit a kidnappers vehicle that is blocking your escape hit at an angle so deflection occurs. Attempt to stay in your vehicle and keep it moving.

Depending where you are in the world kidnapping could be just a usual business risk and nothing more than a regular transaction between local drug lords or gangs and local businesses. In other areas it could mean that your likelihood of survival were negligible. This is once again why planning is critical. You must know this before you decide to act. If you were in the second scenario you know that if kidnapped you are likely to already be considered dead so the risks you take in attempting to get away become less relevant as there is little alternative.

If it's a kidnapping the best chance of your escape is in the first seconds and minutes, when there may be many variables at play and the situation isn't certain. It is also one of the periods of biggest risk. If you see the opportunity to escape or hide then do so but both

of these carry significant risk but on the other hand
so does a kidnapping.

Hostages

Although we have already considered hijacking some of the points cross over with being held hostage. There are a number of cases and instances where you may be held hostage and this can vary in cause from one country to another.

There are however a couple of key points you may consider.

The first is to become anonymous, blend into the group don't stand out, don't become an individual just be part of the group.

Never antagonise your captors, what do you achieve. The US government suggests the following term – Retain a sense of pride but act cooperatively.

Concentrate on surviving. Live another day to get home if possible to the loved ones you care so much about. If you are to be used as a bargaining tool they need to keep you alive.

Be positive look for daylight, small successes and events that may motivate you to keep going.
Be observant. Try and identify patterns, doors that are used, shift patterns, names, numbers you never know what might give you that opportunity to escape or crate an opportunity to live another day.
Remember never attempt to escape unless you are sure of success. This is probably a point of no second chance. Just keep alert and try to find a way of recognising the change of days so you can count your days. It's all part of the game you play in your mind to stay positive.

Try to establish rapport with your captors. This can be difficult as your captors also recognise this approach and can sometimes use this as a cruel trick to destroy your morale.

Recognise that you may be a small cog in a bigger picture and there is little you can do sometimes to affect that. If you think of the hostages in Syria killed very publicly by ISIS then their individual actions had little chance of changing events as they were just a small part of a much bigger picture.

Survive as long as you can. Each day increases your chances of survival. In most cases hostages are not killed.

If you are moved then assume this is your new place of stay settle in and try and use relaxation techniques to cope with the stress. You may be moved repeatedly to help prevent the authorities identifying your location and planning a recovery.

Lastly if an attempt is made to rescue you do not run.

Drop to the floor and stay still, if that is not possible cross your hands on your chest and bow your head.

Don't be upset or alarmed if a rescuer can't decide if you are the captor or the hostage and don't assume they can immediately tell one from the other.

Terrorist Attack

Terrorist attacks cover bomb attacks and shootings as well as hijacking and hostage taking.
Unfortunately as we travel the world there is always an opportunity to fall prey to some kind of terrorist attack. You should always follow your government advice on where not to travel. In the UK the Foreign Office keep up to date information on their website and it's easy and useful to check it before you travel.

Tunisia terrorist attack

An example of everything suddenly going wrong and normal people's lives imploding happened on 19th March 2015 when terrorists in Tunisia attacked leaving 23 dead. Many of the victims were tourists who were visiting the Bardo Museum in Tunis when gunman opened fire. Coaches were shot and people ran for cover in the museum with the gunmen following. This is a typical terrorist situation and sometimes although not in this instance is also coupled with an explosive device. Sometimes the gunfire is used to herd people towards the explosives so the maximum amount of casualties occur.

Interestingly more than 24 hours after the attack in Tunis a Spanish man and his 4 months pregnant wife who were on their honeymoon were found hiding in a small cleaner's room at the museum. They were found after the cruise ship the MSC Splendida realised they had not returned and a search was made of hospitals and then the museum.

This is a perfect example of how to take any small opportunity to stay safe.

Although they were trapped and would have likely been killed had the terrorists found them they did what they could to stay safe. Hiding in a small room is not the best option but it's an option that they had little choice in taking with seconds to decide.

Only later after full investigations would it emerge how many terrorists there were and what areas they had been in. At that specific time none of that was known by this desperate couple. Survival instinct kicked in, they made a decision, acted on it and it saved them.

Vacation

The problem with vacation is that we relax, when we relax we forget the precautions and cares we normally carry around with us.

This relaxation is often coupled with new acquaintances, possibly romances and an increase in the level of alcohol. You can't really get a worse situation than lowered defences alcohol and new acquaintances.

Everything we have discussed earlier applies when on vacation. Nothing changes except your own personal boundaries and approach to the situation around you.

The biggest issue with vacations is that we go to relax and recuperate or have adventures we wouldn't normally undertake. Both of these approaches result in our awareness and caution becoming reduced. Without changing everything around so as to result in the whole purpose of a vacation becoming eroded we can still keep ourselves safe if we take some care and employ some simple precautions.

Wrap Up

In business we identify and recognise risk, assess it and then plan contingencies. Why would you do anything other than this if you look at travel be it business travel or leisure travel.

Run through the contingencies, under different scenarios and try to recognise in advance the situations that can occur, so when they do, you take them in your stride reacting in a way that you would want.

There is only one thing worth risking anything for. It's your life and that of your loved ones. If you are risking your life for anything else you are making a mistake.

If you are fighting to save your wallet or your car then you need to have a word with yourself. Imagine your wife/husband and your children at your graveside as they bury you for dying fighting to save your watch or wallet and hopefully that realism check will make sure that you don't fight for anything else.

One of the games I like to ask people to play is to pretend you are a bodyguard. Only in your mind, please, no jumping across in front of someone like Kevin Costner and Whitney Huston.

As you go about your business for the day and follow the person in front just observe and recognise all the opportunities someone would have to either harm them, rob them or kidnap them. As you move around on your journey don't follow the same person just keep selecting a new person who is in front of you and again run through the game. You will clearly see and identify hundreds of opportunities, now that risk they face could be and is in fact you.

You will see and recognise things you never thought of before. It's not necessary to be paranoid and seem a bit crazy to your colleagues and friends but if you just play the game in your head this repetition of recognising events and risks will start to influence your own behaviours. It's a subtle but highly effective way of slowly developing identification, recognition and mitigations of possible risks.

For further information on training, seminars, presentations and courses please contact the author Tony Willis at the 5 Elements Academy

www.5-elements.co.uk